Passing the Principal

TExES

Exam

To my husband, Greg Wilmore; my children, Brandon Greggory, Brittani Leigh, and Brooke Elaine Wilmore; my mother Irene Watson Litchfield; my late father, Lee Litchfield; and all my friends, colleagues, and students who love and pray for me when I least deserve it. Thank you for being the wind beneath my wings and for always encouraging me to get back up when I fall down. I love you all.

And Jabez prayed to the God of Israel saying,
"Oh, God, please bless me indeed
And enlarge my territory.
May your hand be with me.
Keep me from evil and
Let me not cause pain."
And God honored his request.
I Chronicles 4:10

I can do all things through Christ who strengthens me.
Philippians 4:13

Passing the Principal
TExES
Exam

Keys to
Certification &
School Leadership

Elaine L. Wilmore

CORWIN PRESS, INC.
A Sage Publications Company
Thousand Oaks, California

For information:

 Corwin Press, Inc.
A Sage Publications Company
2455 Teller Road
Thousand Oaks, California 91320
E-mail: order@corwinpress.com

Sage Publications Ltd.
6 Bonhill Street
London EC2A 4PU
United Kingdom

Sage Publications India Pvt. Ltd.
M-32 Market
Greater Kailash I
New Delhi 110 048 India

Printed in the United States of America

A catalog record for this book is available from the Library of Congress.

ISBN 978-0-7619-3986-3

This book is printed on acid-free paper.

09 10   10 9 8 7

Acquisitions Editor: Robb Clouse
Associate Editor: Kylee Liegl
Editorial Assistant: Erin Buchanan
Production Editor: Diane S. Foster
Typesetter: Hespenheide Design
Cover Designer: Michael Dubowe

Contents

Foreword I

I chaired the superintendent's committee on certification standards and am fully familiar with the learner-centered competencies. Elaine Wilmore's *Passing the Principal TExES Examination: Keys to Certification and School Leadership* is a comprehensive guide that meets a great need for aspiring school leaders. It will be beneficial to not only those preparing for principal certification but for the superintendency as well. The book is highly relevant; it will fill any gaps in preparation programs, will compensate for the extensive variations of experience among test takers, and is written in a style that is motivating and affirming.

Dr. Wilmore has hit a home run with *Passing the Principal TExES Examination*. She is a noted authority in school-leadership preparation. In her book, she has achieved an unusual blending of the theoretical with the practical. The content is exactly on target—precisely what aspiring campus leaders need to take them "over the top" on the certification test. The book fills a great void in reliable preparation materials and should not only improve test performance but, more important, improve job performance as well. It is a must-read for all aspiring and current school administrators.

John Horn
Superintendent, Mesquite Independent School District
Former Texas Superintendent of the Year
Horn, Smith, and Wood Consultants

Foreword II

Leadership preparation is like the weather. Lots of people talk about it, but very few do anything about it. In this book, Elaine Wilmore actually sets out to do something about the need for better preparation of school administrators, and she makes the effort for all the right reasons. She is on a quest to change the world.

Better schools mean better communities. In addition, better leadership means better schools. If, in fact, great leadership is the safe harbor in any storm, we need more great leaders. Public education is challenged as never before. We desperately need leaders who can help chart a courageous course of improvement for all schools. Elaine seeks to ensure that we have those needed leaders as she develops the philosophy of student- and community-centered leadership. This book on principal TExES examination preparation is a must-read for those preparing for the exam and for current principals looking to develop collaborative schools and communities. Read, enjoy, and benefit!

Mike Moses
General Superintendent, Dallas Independent School District
Former Texas Commissioner of Education

Preface

Passing the Principal TExES Examination: Keys to Certification and School Leadership was written to help educators in Texas pass the principal Texas Examinations of Educator Standards (TExES). The book is based on domains and competencies provided through Texas law (19 Texas Administrative Code Chapter 241.15) and developed by the Texas State Board for Educator Certification (SBEC). It is written based on the years of experience Wilmore has as a teacher, principal, professor, and school board member teaching at the University of Texas at Arlington and providing popular, successful, and inspiring TExES preparation classes at universities, regional service centers, and other training sites around the state.

The nature of the book is both broad and specific. Part I provides the global overview, tools, and format of the book. Part II provides the philosophy and theoretical framework for TExES success. It details the Texas domains, competencies, and leadership philosophy on which TExES is constructed. Each of Part II's ten chapters details a specific competency in a down-to-earth, interesting manner using real-life stories for practical application while engaging the reader and connecting theory to practice. Each chapter has the details necessary for proactive school leadership and TExES success, and the book closes with an extensive list of additional resources to supplement each domain. Section III ties the philosophy of TExES to other important test-taking concepts and techniques such as how to read and analyze data, manage time while testing, and use specific strategies to discern correct answers. It includes information about how to create an individualized personal success plan, how to prepare for the TExES, and what to do in the weeks, days, and night before the test. The book concludes with a mini-test of applicable decision sets so readers can practice their skills.

Passing the Principal TExES Examination: Keys to Certification and School Leadership is a valued asset for current administrators seeking to refine, refocus, and develop their learner-centered leadership skills as well as helping aspiring administrators pass the TExES examination. It will not only provide a solid theoretical framework for school leadership, it will make learning fun and inspire greatness. Readers will enjoy the book, be ready to pass TExES, and then change the world—one school at a time.

Acknowledgments

Writing this book has been my dream for a long time. My sincerest thank-you to everyone at Corwin Press, especially Robb Clouse, the acquisitions editor, for facilitating its coming true and for being so exceedingly nice about the process. My family has been unbelievable through this strenuous writing period. My husband, Greg, and my dean at the University of Texas at Arlington, Dr. Jeanne M. Gerlach, have encouraged me, even prodded me, for years to do this. Thank you to you both. When it was obvious that I would need quiet time to write, Greg did everything in his power to protect me from the world's worst interrupter—the telephone. He has really been great in every way. For 29 years his dreams for me have always been higher than those I have had for myself. Thank you, Greg, for believing in me and making me stretch.

The same is true for the rest of my family. My mother, Irene Litchfield, lives with us. She has been so patient when I would disappear into our library for long hours. When Greg would come home I could hear her say, "Elaine's upstairs. I haven't seen her all day. She's still working." At age 88 my mother is the perfect blend and role model of an intelligent, independent, "aim for the best," feisty, witty, sharp-as-a-tack parent. I love you, Mother, and I miss you, Daddy. Thank you for being such great parents.

My children are the best. They also have encouraged me and been so good about the time I have spent at the computer. There is Brandon, who like Greg and Jeanne, has encouraged me: "You need to write books, Mom!" There is Brooke who has asked about ten zillion times, "Are you still on the computer, Mom??" And, what would I have done without Brittani? Brittani graduated from Texas A&M this May and has spent her time off before starting her new job doing major edits for me on this book. There is absolutely no way I could have finished without her. My truest gratitude and love to each of you. You are the best family anyone could ever have.

Thank you also to the entire department of Educational Leadership and Policy Studies at the University of Texas at Arlington (UTA) and especially to Dr. Jesse Jai McNeil Jr., my colleague and dear friend. Together we have built programs to make lots of people's dreams come true. Thank you to all the past, present, and future UTA students who have inspired me with their passion and zeal and who have heeded my call to go forth and change the world. Thank you for your *constant* affirmation and support, for how you always are there with your bright faces, ready to learn, and never seeming to complain that I am likely the oddest, most "out-of-the-box" professor you ever could have

xiv   PASSING THE PRINCIPAL TExES EXAM

imagined. Instead, you always lift me up. A graduating class recently called me their "Dorothy" from the *Wizard of Oz*, always seeking to guide their hearts toward home. I promise to never give up trying and to always be your zealot.

I have so many friends to thank that I do not know where to start. These are people who also have given me so much encouragement to get my message out there. They have seen me at my worst and love me anyway; friends who celebrate with me when I am happy, weep with me when I am sad, and pray for me when I am so tired and my shoulder hurts. There are many more, but I must acknowledge N. C. Woolverton Jr.; JoNell and Larry Jones; Kathy and Dr. Joe Martin; Helen and Wes Nelson, Renea, Dr. Wade, and Emily Smith; Donna and Milton Walker, Wanda and John Rollen; Billie Westbrook; Dr. Joannie Atkinson; Bill Stewart; Kerry VanDoren Pedigo; and my oldest, lifelong friend, Melda Cole Ward.

Last, to John R. Hoyle and David A. Erlandson at Texas A&M University. Thank you for all you mean in my life. I made a vow years ago to try to make you proud. I hope this book does it.

" . . . saying, I am Alpha and Omega, the first and the last: and, What thou seest, write in a book, . . ."

Revelation 1:11

All my love,
Elaine

About the Author

Elaine L. Wilmore, PhD, is an Associate Professor in the department of Educational Leadership and Policy Studies at the University of Texas at Arlington (UTA), President of Elaine L. Wilmore Leadership Initiatives, and President-Elect of the National Council of Professors of Educational Administration. She is the UTA founding Director of School Administration Programs, Educational Leadership UTA, and the Scholars of Practice, innovative programs for which she has received multiple state and private foundation grants. She has also served as Chair of Educational Administration and Director of University Program Development and is currently Chair of the UTA School of Education Faculty Advisory Committee. Dr. Wilmore is active on many local, state, and national boards. These currently include serving on the Executive Board of the National Council Professors of Educational Administration, the Texas Principals Leadership Initiative, the Texas Consortium of Colleges of Teacher Education, and others. She has served as a program/folio reviewer for the Educational Leadership Constituent Council for the National Council for the Accreditation of Teacher Education. Dr. Wilmore is known in Texas for her statewide success in helping students pass administrative certification examinations.

Dr. Wilmore is a former public school teacher, counselor, and elementary and middle school principal. She is in her second term on the Cleburne Independent School District Board of Trustees, where she serves as vice president. A frequent national speaker and writer, Dr. Wilmore is known for inspiring others to greatness. In addition to her significant work in the area of administrator development, she enjoys singing in her church choir. She is married and the mother of three wonderful children, a big boxer dog, and a mutt-cat named Yum.

I

Content

The Knowledge Base

Welcome!

In the state of Texas, as in many other states, there is a rigorous certification examination that potential administrators must pass before they are eligible for certification. In Texas this test is called the TExES (Texas Examinations of Educator Standards). There is tremendous pressure on future leaders to pass this test. Without it, they cannot become certified. There is also tremendous pressure on preparation programs for their students to do well. Potential test takers from both inside and outside the state are looking for tools to help them achieve their goal of certification and reaching the principalship. This book describes how to become the world's best principal through awesome leadership preparation.

Universities and alternative preparation programs are working hard to address both the knowledge and the philosophical bases on which TExES is framed. The test is built on a foundation of nine competencies within three domains, and its creators assume that test takers have received knowledge and research preparation through their educational providers. This book will supply needed supplemental resources for the knowledge base, but it is not intended to substitute for a master's degree. It will focus, however, on the philosophy necessary to "think" like a learner-centered principal. Many students find it difficult to make the transition from thinking like a teacher to thinking, reflecting, reacting, and responding like a principal. All of the knowledge in the world is useless if a test taker cannot "think" in the way the test was developed. *Passing the Principal TExES Examination: Keys to Certification and School Leadership* addresses the philosophy as well as the skills that principals must have within each of the three domains and nine competencies. It provides test-taking tips for before, during, and after the exam. Specific attention is given to in-state and out-of-state test takers. The volume also provides practice test questions grouped into "decision sets" within a "mini-test." Each competency chapter concludes with additional resources that will be helpful to students as they develop the knowledge and philosophical bases necessary to pass the test and pursue careers as lifelong learners.

Finally, this book is written in an informal, first-person voice. There will be real-life stories and applications integrated into each competency to help the reader tie concepts to reality. It is absolutely necessary that test takers apply their knowledge and skills to the test—as well as to life in general. In a friendly, supportive manner, *Passing the Principal TExES Examination* will help test takers and others interested in learner-centered leadership integrate TExES competencies and domains into real-world application. Let's see how.

Basic Concepts

The principal TExES is divided into three domains with nine competencies. These domains are as follows:

- School community leadership
- Instructional leadership
- Administrative leadership

There are three competencies within school community leadership, four within instructional leadership, and two within administrative leadership. Questions on the test are designed to address specific competencies. They are not evenly divided, however. Approximately 33% of the questions address competencies within school community leadership. Approximately 44% address different competencies from instructional leadership. The final 22% focus on administrative leadership. There are no absolute numbers of questions per competency or domain. My goal is for *all* my students to get *all* the questions correct, regardless of which domain or competency a question comes from. Nonetheless, a student does not have to score 100% to pass the test. For many students, simply realizing they do not have to earn a perfect score on the test helps to take off some of the pressure, and this is a benefit because half the battle of passing this test is a mind game. In other words, you must know that you can and will succeed. It is my intention for everyone reading this book to win the mind game. You should walk in to take the test feeling cool, calm, collected, confident—and even downright cocky; you should walk out feeling the same. This mental attitude is necessary to lower your level of stress. When your stress level goes up, your productivity goes down (see Figure 1.1). We want your stress level down and your productivity to be way up. Therefore, you should be cool, calm, collected, confident, and downright cocky throughout both your preparation and the test-taking experience.

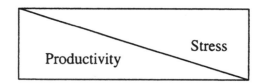

Figure 1.1. Productivity Stays Up When Stress Goes Down

Many people place great emphasis on figuring out exactly which competency each question addresses. Although I discuss this strategy, it does not receive undue attention. Remember, if our goal is to get every question correct, why do we care from which competency the question came? We do not; we want to get all the questions right. Nonetheless, upon becoming thoroughly familiar with each of the competencies, as you will by reading Chapters 3 through 11, you will recognize key words and concepts that will guide your selection of the appropriate answers to get all the questions right—or at least enough questions right to pass.

In addition, there is significant overlap of key themes within the competencies. Since the test is largely a timed mind game, why would you want to get stressed out, with the clock ticking, by worrying if a question is addressing competency 001 or 003? Who cares? The important thing is to understand, integrate, and live the competencies. Make them your "school administrator's bible." Beginning this minute, let your walk match your talk in modeling these competencies in your daily life. Then on the day of the test, walk in there and ace TExES because you are already "walking the talk!"

Leadership: A Skill or an Art?

There has been, and likely always will be, considerable discussion of whether good leadership is a skill that can be studied or an art that is practiced as diligently as master painters practice their own art form, working hard to produce a masterpiece. For years, researchers such as Kent Peterson, Lee Bolman, and Terrence Deal have presented a view of school leadership that blends concepts of skill and art. Indeed, leadership is a blend of art and skill. Skills are absolutely necessary for good leadership, but they must be practiced and nurtured into the nuances of an art. Never forget that leadership is a talent. Develop it. Nurture it in yourself and in others. Your school, as well as you personally and others whom your leadership affects, will benefit.

Think of leadership as a really good jazz band. As the musicians practice before a performance, they individually sound like a whole lot of noise. They are all doing their own thing, warming up, and getting ready for the concert. But once the performance begins, everything comes together. The musicians play as a team. They are people who have worked hard, practiced together, and who have the common goal of producing really beautiful music. Because they have done those things, the concert begins, and their skills turn into an art as they blend together, bending and flowing with the crescendos and decrescendos, the tempo, and the dynamics of the music to produce something truly beautiful.

Our schools deserve leaders that are orchestrating a wonderful jazz band. As long as everyone in the school is doing their own thing, independent of each other, it is just noise. Although some progress may be made, everyone's skills are acting independently. They are not making beautiful music. But with a great leader—a learner-centered leader with passion, vision, and purpose—the school of musicians can win a Grammy. Every child in every school deserves to be a part of that jazz band, the jazz band that produces artful music, not noise. Every child deserves to be a part of a learning team. Every child deserves to be a part of a school that is focused on their success in every facet of their lives. Every child deserves the chance to come away a winner.

For too many students today, there is little hope for the future. It is my goal that you become the leader of your school's jazz band. You will be the leader that does what is right instead of what is easy or bureaucratic. You will be the principal that facilitates your school in developing a common vision and a solid purpose built on identified common values. You will be the one to change the world . . . or at least your campus. You will become an awesome principal, or I will come back and haunt you.

But first, you must pass the TExES. Are you ready to get started?

Getting Started

Section II of this book includes Chapters 2 through 11. Chapter 2, "The Big Picture," provides the global view of how you will achieve your goal of passing the test. This test is merely a gatekeeper designed to see that you have a specific learner-centered philosophy of school leadership as portrayed in the domains and competencies. It requires entry-level administrative skills and expectations, and it is a passable test. You *will* pass this test.

I teach school leadership at the University of Texas at Arlington. I also teach TExES preparation classes all over the state. It brings me great joy when students from any of them contact me to let me know they passed the test. I get really excited! After all, that means there is one more human out there ready to join my journey toward improving the world. And when you pass, you can send me chocolate (plain Hershey bars, please), roses (I prefer pink), or ice cream (only Blue Bell, of course). Chapters 3 through 11 give detailed attention to each of the nine learner-centered competencies. If you have never even heard of them up to this point, that is all right. By the time I get through with you, you will be living and breathing them. If not, you are in a coma. Check with your doctor. It is time to wake up to get ready for this test. You are going to know those competencies inside out. You will be reciting them to your families and friends. If you do not have family or friends, I strongly suggest finding some. They will be a great support system—and they'll be there to celebrate when you pass the test!

Section III addresses the integration and application of all you have learned in Section II. You will become skilled at how to analyze data, learn specific test-taking strategies, create your own Personal Success Plan, and then tie it all together in Chapter 15, "From Now Until Eternity." Finally, the book concludes with a mini-test similar to the structure of the real test. By the time you walk in to take TExES, you will be so well prepared that all you will want to do is go in and pass it so you can go forward to improve the world and eat more chocolate. This test is just a nuisance to get in your way until then. So, let's get rid of the nuisance by passing the test.

Are you ready? Let's go!

II

Philosophy
The Theoretical Framework

The Big Picture

Global Overview of TExES Domains

It is helpful to understand "the big picture" of the theoretical framework—that is, the competencies and domains—on which TExES is built before we get into the details of the competencies. As introduced in Chapter 1, the nine competencies are placed into three domains: school community leadership, instructional leadership, and administrative leadership. There is significant overlap in the integration of the individual competencies because a principalship is not a segmented, compartmentalized job. Daily roles and tasks overlap. While fighting the fires of a normal school day, does the average principal stop to ask, "Gee, I wonder if I should respond through Competency 002 or 006?" Definitely not! This is why you should know the competencies inside and out and internalize their concepts so that you can respond reflectively and instinctively. Before getting into the detailed analysis of the competencies within Chapters 3 through 11, let us discuss specific components in format and the theoretical framework of the domains.

Key Concepts

I provide three key concepts per domain to help you identify and keep them straight—both as you prepare for the test and afterward as you grow as a principal. These key words will capture the basic essence of what each domain is about. They will help you focus as you dig deeper into the concepts they represent in the competencies. During the test, the concepts they represent will serve as clues to identifying the right answers.

Guess My Favorites

Each competency chapter will feature my personal favorites among the domains and competencies. By anticipating ahead of time which ones they are, you will internalize the thought process of the test as well as synthesize what the concepts stand for. It isn't that you really care which are my favorites. This is simply a strategy to help you internalize the philosophy of the test that is necessary for success. During the discussion of the domains in this chapter, I tell you which is my favorite as a preview to the competencies. In Chapters 3 through 11, I don't tell you my favorites until after the discussion. Consider it a game. See if you can figure out which are my favorites before I tell you. If you can, you're off to a great start in that competency. You will also be on your way toward becoming a learner-centered principal.

The Ideal Principal

For just a few minutes, stop and close your eyes. Visualize in your mind an ideal principal whom you know or with whom you have worked. If you cannot think of an ideal principal, make one up. Perhaps your person will be a combination of the skills or talents of several different principals that you know or wish you knew. Think about all the things this real or imaginary person does or could do. What makes her or him great? What attributes or characteristics does this principal have? What makes the person better than the average principal? What makes this principal outstanding? Take a few minutes to really think about this. *Do not blow off this exercise!*

After you open your eyes, write on a piece of paper the adjectives or other words you used to describe this ideal principal in your mind. Take several minutes to do this. At first, obvious characteristics will come to your mind. Fine. Write them down.

When you think you have thought of them all, dig a little deeper. Come up with some more. It is in this deep reflection that you will get to the heart of the traits of the ideal principal. List 20 to 30. You can do it! Dig deep and come up with some more really good ones. Write them down.

If possible, prepare for the test with a friend. Study and discuss this book together. Do this exercise together. Then compare your results. Your results will multiply as you collaborate. You will likely have identified many common characteristics, and that's fine. Great principals *do* have many things in common. However, you and your friend may also have come up with different characteristics. Are they things you can agree on? Are they things you both agree constitute this new "mega-ideal principal"? Come up with a master list of characteristics of the ideal principal. Discuss them together. Keep this composite to review periodically before the test. Why did you select these traits and not others? Elaborate on your thought process. This is what becoming a reflective practitioner is all about. This exercise is worth true effort, and it will help you pass the test.

Once you have developed your ideal principal, think about that principal and no other for the rest of your life. Think about that person as you study the domains and competencies. Think about the ideal principal as you are selecting responses to the practice "decision set" questions you will find at the end of this book. Above all, think only about the ideal principal on the day you take TExES. Do not think, "That's unreasonable," or "That response isn't practical." Forget reasonable and practical! Think ideal! You can be reasonable and practical when you are picking out a new car. On test day, think *ideal principal!* Think, "Dr. Wilmore says, 'Forget reasonable and practical. Think ideal!'" There are enough reasonable and practical principals out there who have totally lost sight of the vision and purpose of the school. Think ideal to change the world—one student and school at a time. Besides, what you learn from this book will haunt you if you ever turn into a bureaucrat.

Pretend

Remember when you were a child and played pretend games? It was fun to pretend to be an astronaut or president of the United States. (You're never too old to play make-believe!) Well, let's play the Pretend Game again. Let's say that you are not into this whole "ideal principal" concept. Let's say that thinking "ideal" is just too far-fetched and would never work in the real world. Let's say that you cannot think of a single good reason to hold the ideal principal up as a standard for making TExES exam answer choices.

Pretend. You believe you can become an ideal principal and really affect your school. Imagine how you would feel if this were so. Savor that feeling and work toward it forever.

There is no law that says you have to believe in any of the traits of the ideal principal. Maybe your goal in life is to be a bureaucrat. If this is true, I have suggestions:

1. On the day of the test, pretend like crazy! You may not buy the philosophy of the ideal principal, but I can guarantee one thing. The developers of this test do, and they hold all the cards. Therefore, if you want to pass this test, pretend like crazy.
2. What if you can't do it? You simply do not buy one word of this "ideal principal" concept. You really *do* want to become a bureaucrat. You have a burning desire to sit in the principal's office listening to Mozart, doing as little as possible, and never actually become invested in the lives of others. Nonetheless, you'd like to look important while you do nothing. Here's my suggestion. Put away this book. It will do nothing for you except raise your blood pressure.

You've learned the way you're supposed to think to pass this test and change the world, and you've learned to pretend on test day—that is, if you have difficulty with the concept of the ideal principal. Now it's time to get started with the three domains.

The Three Domains

Domain I: School Community Leadership

Key Words: Culture, Climate, and Vision

Domain I is *school community leadership.* Approximately 33% of the test is from this domain. I love this domain. It is my personal favorite. It likely will not take you long to figure out why.

In a nutshell, school community leadership concentrates on all the things a principal should do to develop and nurture a culture, climate, and vision of the school that is supportive of all stakeholders and helps them succeed. Who is a stakeholder? Everyone. Absolutely no one is left out. Stakeholders go hand-in-hand with another key TExES term and concept: the *learning community* or *school community.* The idea is to get everyone possible involved in identifying common values, developing a shared purpose and vision of the school, and developing goals and strategies to achieve them. The school community consists of teachers, counselors, paraprofessionals, auxiliary personnel, parents, community members, businesses, churches, and everyone else interested in the school. The more people you can get involved, the better. People support what they help build. Our schools need all the help and support they can get.

You may ask, "What if my school is the pits? What if it is located in a part of town where no one wants to go? It is dangerous. The idea of getting parents or anyone else involved is pretty far-fetched." Fine. Think far-fetched. Remember, we are focused on the ideal principal. The ideal principal learned at the feet of Winston Churchill. During the bleakest moments of World War II, Churchill was known for telling the English that their nation would never, never give up. England never did give up. Eventually, the Allies won the war, preserving freedom and democracy for the next generation. It did not happen by taking the easy road or rolling over and playing dead. It happened through hard work, perseverance, and collaboration with other countries.

The same is true within Domain I. The ideal principal will never give up. It doesn't matter how bleak the circumstances; ideal principals pick themselves up, dust themselves off, and start all over again. It takes intense resiliency to be a great school principal. Anyone can be a lackluster, status quo principal. Who on Earth needs more of those? Certainly not us! We are Domain I principals, intent on facilitating that everyone collaborate for a better tomorrow. It's a vision thing. Never give up. Never.

Can you see why this domain is my favorite?

Domain II: Instructional Leadership

Key Words: Curriculum, Instruction, and Staff Development

Domain II is the "meat and potatoes" of the principalship. It is what makes us different from chief executive officers or managers of any other organization. We are here to lead schools, not shoe stores. What are we selling? Curriculum and instruction. How do we do that? Through improved staff development. Notice, I did not say *teacher* development. That would be limiting. We do not want to limit anything or anyone. Motivational speaker Les Brown says to reach for the moon. Even if you do not reach it, you will land among the stars. Awesome principals want to nurture and develop everyone. They reach for the moon and settle for the stars only if they have to. Landing among the stars sure beats being in the pits, however.

Always dream big. I tell my students that if they do not remember one other thing that I teach them, to remember to dream big dreams. I even have it on my university voice mail. You would be surprised how many people leave messages commenting about what a surprise it is to hear anyone encouraging them to "dream big." I always wonder, isn't dreaming big what universities are all about?

In fact, isn't that what all schools are for? Domain II is about improving curriculum and instruction for the benefit of all students. It's about finding ways to nurture and develop staff members so they can be the arms and legs for improved curriculum and instruction, to meet the developmental needs of all students.

This would be a good time to introduce TAAS—the Texas Assessment of Academic Skills. For out-of-state test takers, TAAS is a really big test in Texas. Students begin taking it in the third grade. They keep taking it until they pass the high school version. If students do not pass the high school TAAS, they do not graduate, period. It doesn't matter if they make straight A's. It doesn't matter how many honors or advanced placement classes they have taken. It doesn't matter if they have a wonderful scholarship waiting for them. They must pass that test. Students who fail TAAS in the early grades are identified as "at risk." Plans are made to remediate them so they will pass the following year, to help get them on track for the high school exam. The public schools of Texas are under intense pressure for students to do well on TAAS. The state accountability system is directly linked to student success or failure on TAAS. The TExES refers to TAAS many times. It is not the purpose of this book to address whether TAAS is a good thing or a bad thing. It doesn't matter—it's the law. And if it's the law, then it's the hand we're dealt. And if it's the hand we're playing, you can guess what we must do. *Win!*

If we think of TAAS as a game that we intend to win, we must become coaches and produce game plans and strategies to make sure we do. How many coaches do you know that say, "Well, guys, it's Friday night in Texas. Half the town will be out there waiting to see you play. They don't really care if you win or lose. They just want to see you looking good in those great uniforms." Right. In *Texas?* I don't think so. In Texas, teams are expected to win. If they do not, serious things can happen. It is downright un-Texan!

Domain II is about winning. Think "curriculum, instruction, and staff development." Our tools for winning are curriculum, instruction, and staff development. They are our game plan. They are the "meat and potatoes" of who we are and why we are here. To create a better world, we must have an educated society. Meat and potatoes. Curriculum, instruction, and staff development. Domain II. Think winning!

Domain III: Administrative Leadership

Key Words: Resources, Facilities, and Safety

The third domain, administrative leadership, is different from the first two. Domain I deals with the culture, climate, and vision of the school. Domain II deals with the "meat and potatoes," the staples of schooling that are curriculum, instruction, and staff development. Domain III takes a slightly different direction. It deals with the business of running the school. It is absolutely necessary that principals are committed and passionate about the campus vision and that they do everything possible to augment appropriate curriculum and instruction. Still, if principals cannot appropriately manage the daily operations of their schools, ultimately they will not be successful.

Domain III deals with budget, resource allocation, financial management, personnel management, facilities, and safety. For principals to be effective, they must provide a balance of leadership and management skills. It won't matter if you are passionate about meeting the needs of all students if you cannot plan for and allocate funds properly. Your central business office will take action if you continually run with a deficit. They may be kind about it once or twice, but if the problem continues, they will not be so understanding. If you do not "get your act together" financially, they will see to it that you don't have that problem anymore because you will no longer be the principal. This will not help the cause of proactive change agents, so Domain III is very important.

There is one specific aspect of Domain III that bears emphasis here, as well as within subsequent chapters. That is the issue of school safety. We used to think of school safety as having a safe facility, with access for the disabled, safe playgrounds, and the right number of fire, tornado, or other emergency drills. Unfortunately, our world has moved far beyond that. With school shootings such as at Columbine High School in Colorado—and even church shootings such as the one at Wedgwood in Fort Worth—violence has infiltrated the two most sacred institutions in the United States: our places of worship and the places where we educate our young. This is wrong, and there is no way to justify it.

But it is also reality. To ignore the fact that violence is occurring would be to hide our heads in the sand. Positive, change-agent principals never hide their heads in the sand. They are always looking ahead by having practiced emergency plans in place. Furthermore, in their proactivity these principals are constantly vigilant of signs that students or others are in need, and they work to meet those needs so that a school's emergency plan will never be put into action.

In the spring of 2001, Santana High School in Southern California experienced school violence. Just a few weeks later, an additional high school in the same district was struck by violence. At the time, reporters interviewed school officials. They said they had a plan for violence intervention. Teachers, students, police, and everyone else involved worked the plan. They did everything they were supposed to do. What concerned the principal, however, was what triggered the need to put the plan into action. This is the hard part.

The ideal principal never gives up. The ideal principal works constantly, without letting up, to maintain a safe and effective learning environment for all students. Anything less is simply going through the motions.

You have now been introduced to the global view of the three learner-centered domains. The next nine chapters delve into the specificity of the nine competencies that fall within these three domains. From the beginning you will know that if a competency—or a test question—has something to do with vision, climate, or culture, it is likely a Domain I question. You should look for a test response that also directly relates to the same issue. The same is true for the other two domains. To keep your domains straight, remember your key concepts.

Remember as well that sometimes the TExES provides what seems to be an excellent answer choice but that doesn't answer the question to which it refers. Underline important words in the prompt and question to keep you focused on exactly what is asked. If the test gives you a wonderful selection choice, but it doesn't apply to the question and isn't in line with the appropriate domain, forget it. It may be beautiful, but it isn't the right answer to the question. Now let's take a look at those nine competencies.

Learner-Centered Leadership and Campus Culture

Domain I: School Community Leadership

Domain Key Concepts: Culture, Climate, Vision

Competency 001

The principal knows how to shape campus culture by facilitating the development, articulation, implementation, and stewardship of a vision of learning that is shared and supported by the school community.

If I could pick one specific competency out of all nine that was my favorite, this would be the one. It sums up my personal philosophy of school leadership. We will discuss it in detail not just because it is my favorite, but because there is significant overlapping of key concepts between the nine competencies. Once we have our philosophical framework laid out with 001, it will integrate into the other eight.

As we begin looking at the competencies, be careful to watch for the verbs. They are always action verbs. They also say a lot about the philosophy of leadership necessary to pass the TExES and to provide learner-centered leadership, as you are busy changing the world, one school at a time. This competency begins with the principal's shaping, not dictating, campus culture. This is vital. Throughout the competencies, you'll see the principal as a leader who shapes, facilities, develops, nurtures, and supports the school and community. The old "top-down" leadership and management style is not manifest in this framework. We are looking not at tyrants, but at nurturing, supportive principals. Therefore, right off the bat, our principal is shaping the campus culture by facilitating:

- Development
- Articulation
- Implementation
- Stewardship of a vision of learning

To understand these four points, it is important first to understand the entire concept of vision. Vision is not where our school currently is. It is where we want it to be. Our vision should make us reach for the moon. It should represent what our school could be if we really believe that miracles can happen and that we can change whatever is necessary to make our school the best it can be. Our vision is the ideal school.

Vision is not our individual vision. It is the collaboratively developed campus vision that is developed by lots of people working together, brainstorming ideas of "wouldn't it be nice if we could . . ." and then making plans to see to it that those things happen. Our vision is our dream. It is the way we yearn for our schools to be. Visions will vary in specifics from school to school and district to district. All schools are different. The point is not the differences between campus visions. The point is that all schools have a vision; they all have goals, strategies, resources, and time lines to facilitate the development of the vision, and they have an accountability system to ensure the vision becomes a reality.

Visions are marked by passion and commitment. They are never laissez-faire. They shoot for the top with a sincere belief in achievement. If you aim high, even if you do not reach your goals, you'll get farther then you would if you had aimed lower. So having a vision of what your school could be rather than what it is becomes very important.

It is also important to involve as many people as possible in developing the vision and subsequent goals and strategies to achieve them. The school community includes everyone interested in the success of the campus. It is more than just teachers and administrators. It is parents, paraprofessionals, auxiliary staff, cafeteria workers, bus drivers, neighbors, businesses, churches —everyone who cares or does not care about the school. Involve them all. In fact, it is quite important to attempt to involve those who are resistant to change or openly nonsupportive of the school because it is human nature to support what you have helped build. Get those naysayers in there. Involve them. When they criticize, let them come up with ideas to solve the situation. It won't happen overnight, but if you're patient, exceedingly calm, and treat these people with respect, eventually they will become a part of the team. Lyndon Johnson used to say that he wanted to know who his enemies were so he could keep them close at hand. In schools, we want to involve our "enemies," the people who give us the most grief, in helping develop a better way for all our students to be successful. Bring them in, give them a job, and reward their efforts with respect and appreciation. Be persistent and consistent. Exercise pure grit. The goal is to make everyone part of the school community team for student success.

Having said all this about vision, let us look again at the four points we want to develop. An ideal principal works hard to collaboratively develop the vision in the ways we just discussed, by empowering many different types of people in the brainstorming process. Having a vision alone will not take the school where it needs to be if it is not articulated appropriately. The articulation of the vision is the communication and marketing of it. You may say that you did not enter education to be in sales, but guess what? If you do not think we should be selling our schools, take a good look at the growth of private, charter, and home schools. There is a reason for that. Private and charter schools know the value of articulating their mission. They believe in their cause. If they do not, their doors close. Public schools need to do a much better job of marketing the good news of student success that is occurring on virtually every campus. Bad news always travels fast. Good news does not. It is our responsibility to get out there and be the best cheerleaders for the value of education that the world has ever seen. Does this mean that we will always agree on everything? Of course not. Conflict is necessary for growth to occur; otherwise we remain stuck in the status quo we are trying to escape. There are times that we must agree to disagree but then go forth with a united front. No matter how much discourse went into the development of the vision, when it comes to articulation, the entire school community must speak with one voice. You cannot blow an uncertain trumpet. Everyone must articulate the same vision and the same message—with the same passion and commitment.

Next comes the implementation of the vision. It is one thing to develop and articulate goals, strategies, and an accountability network. It is something else to implement it—to put it into place. This is where we put the pedal to the metal to get the thing done. There is no more talking about it in future tense. We all know people who can talk a good line but cannot walk their talk. These are the people less suited to implement a vision. Conversely, there are those who have difficulty showing outward enthusiasm but who truly are committed to and passionate about the campus cause. These are the master implementers. They are the "worker bees," the ones we need to really get the job done. Nurture these folks!

So we have collaboratively developed our vision. We have *articulated* it far and wide. We have *implemented* it. What is this *stewardship* business?

The stewardship of a vision is imperative. It is also very dear to my heart. This is the "feeding of the flock," the flock being the school community. Sometimes we can work to get an idea or project going. People can be committed, motivated, and hardworking. But as time goes by, reality hits—and reality is not always fun. It's easy to lose your enthusiasm when you are just plain tired. Morale can really be affected when people get totally worn out physically, psychologically, or emotionally. All these factors can be damaging, and the campus will be affected.

This is why the stewardship of a vision is so critically important. Everyone has times, days, and circumstances when things just aren't going right. No matter what we do or how hard we try, things are all wrong. Nothing we do seems to help. The people we try to help or please do not seem like they want to be helped or pleased. In fact, it seems as if their goal in life is to be miserable and bring everyone around them down with them. Such negativity will obviously affect the culture and the climate of the school. Something must be done.

This is why the stewardship of the vision is so critical. The role of the principal is to become the shepherd of the flock. You must find the ways and resources to tend, nurture, and support everyone who is a part of the vision while always seeking to involve more people. You must provide an ear, a shoulder, and a heart to prove you are interested, concerned, and definitely involved with the situation. It is the role of the principal, as steward of the vision, to help people get back up when they fall. This may be the most difficult thing for a principal to do day after day because someone is always down. That is the nature of life. Being there, being connected physically and emotionally to your school, supporting the vision, facilitating resources and success, helping people get back up when they are down, and continuously helping them to grow better is critically important to the success of the school. It is also a difficult component of being an awesome school administrator. Usually, when you support someone when they are down or when they've made a mistake, they will do the same for you when your turn comes. We are all human, and we all make mistakes. In the ideal school, we are a family working together. We make mistakes, but we get over them. We solve problems and go on because we have a united purpose. That purpose is our vision. Nurture it and sustain it. It holds our future.

The Principal Knows How To . . .

- *Create a campus culture that sets high expectations, promotes learning, and provides intellectual stimulation for self, students, and staff members.*

Campus culture is critical to the success of the school. The culture of any organization determines what is valued. In this instance, the culture values high expectations, promotes learning, and provides intellectual stimulation. This does not say pretty good expectations. It says high expectations. It does not say to promote learning and provide intellectual stimulation just for the easy to teach, the well behaved, or those who speak English fluently. It says for self, students, and staff members. This means everyone, and everyone is a cousin to *all*, which is a popular TExES term and concept. Watch for it. Be careful to notice that *intellectual stimulation* includes *self*. Just because you become certified as an administrator does not mean that your intellectual stimulation is over. Absolutely not! It's just beginning! Great principals are role models for letting their walk match their talk. If they want their schools to be intellectually stimulating, they must be intellectually stimulating themselves. Someone is always watching.

- *Ensure that parents and other members of the community are an integral part of the campus culture.*

The key concepts here are *ensure* and *an integral part. Ensure* means to guarantee, make sure it happens, not to hope it happens or to wish it would not. This point does not say that parents and other members of the community are to be tolerated, ignored, or treated condescendingly. It says they are an integral part of the campus culture. Be sure parents and every member of your school community is welcomed, appreciated, and respected at all times, even when they do not act as if they deserve it. That's when they need it the most!

- *Implement strategies to ensure the development of collegial relationships and effective collaboration.*

There are three important concepts here. First, to implement strategies, collaborative planning must have previously occurred. You cannot effectively implement anything that has not been developed and articulated as part of the vision of the school. Second, watch the word *ensure* again. Finally, the development of collegial relationships and effective collaboration is essential to the culture and climate of the school. These things do not happen by chance. They happen because they have been planned for, nurtured, and sustained as part of the stewardship of the vision. What steps would the ideal principal take as a school leader to facilitate collegial relationships and effective collaboration? If there are not collegial relationships, it does not take a Rhodes Scholar to realize there will not be effective collaboration. The school community should be a family, pulling together to achieve common goals at all times. As with biological families, sometimes things will not go perfectly. Sometimes family members will be tired, discouraged, disheartened, frustrated, cranky, or just plain wrong. But they are still members of our family. We love and support them, helping pick them up and start over and work toward a better day tomorrow.

The same should be true in our schools. No one is perfect all the time. Everyone falls down. To have collegial relationships we pick each other up, dust each other off, and nurture and encourage each other. Things will be all right if we stick together and don't give up. Perseverance pays. With these types of collegial relationships, a natural development is effective collaboration. Both are necessary for our schools to maximize student opportunity and learning in a supportive campus climate.

- *Respond appropriately to diverse needs in shaping the campus culture.*

Positive, proactive principals know this and respond appropriately to the diverse needs of different types of students, parents, faculty, staff members, and communities. All people and needs are a part of the campus culture. Students live, learn, and react differently. So do communities. This is a different world than it was a generation ago. Embrace it. Cherish it. Love it. Respond appropriately to it. The future of our democratic society depends on it.

- *Use various types of information (e.g., demographic data, campus climate inventory results, student achievement data, emerging issues affecting education) to develop a campus vision and create a plan for implementing the vision.*

There is a concept represented here, *triangulation,* that you will remember from your research classes. Triangulation simply means using multiple sources of data to gather input, verify results, and draw conclusions in data driven decision making. Although the word itself is not used in the competencies, the concept it represents is used over and over. They want you to use multiple sources of data in every type of decision-making process.

In this case, the various types of information, with examples provided, should be used to develop a campus vision and create a plan for implementing the vision. As we have discussed repeatedly, the development of a campus vision is absolutely essential to campus success. It is the common denominator of everything we do. It is our daily focus. It is where we look when we are discouraged. It is there to lift us up, to refocus us on where we are going and why we are here. Without a clearly defined and articulated campus vision, we are not what we should be, which is a definite disservice to our school community. If we take our eyes off our vision and are unable or unwilling to refocus, it is time to hang it up, take a leave of absence, or quit. Do anything else, but do not inflict a bad attitude on students and teachers. It is your responsibility to lift others up. To do this, you must be clearly focused and committed to the campus vision. You certainly must know what that vision is and be able to clearly articulate it.

Having the vision and commitment is not enough. You must create a plan for implementing the vision. How is this done? It is accomplished through collaborative collegial relationships with all members of the school community. Again, this is not something that is quickly and easily thrown together in an afterschool faculty meeting. It is something that is developed, implemented, and nurtured over time. The school must have a plan and work the plan for implementing the vision.

- *Use strategies for involving all stakeholders in planning processes to enable the collaborative development of a shared campus vision focused on teaching and learning.*

If our shared campus vision is not focused on teaching and learning, then we have serious problems. It must be focused on specific and detailed strategies. These strategies must involve all stakeholders in planning processes. If all stakeholders are involved in the planning processes, it enables collaborative development of a shared vision. The important point to remember here is that there be involvement of all stakeholders in the planning and use of strategies to reach the campus vision. The vision does not occur by happenstance. It develops and evolves through hard work, collaboration, planning, development, and implementation of specific strategies designed to make sure the vision occurs successfully. Have a plan. Work the plan. Assess the plan. Modify the plan. Do everything it takes, but make sure you have a plan!

- *Facilitate the collaborative development of a plan that clearly articulates objectives and strategies for implementing a campus vision.*

This is similar to the previous concept. The word *facilitate* makes clear the point that the principal's effort alone cannot reach the school community's goals. That would not be collaborative. Collaborative principals empower others by facilitating success. People support what they help build. Therefore, you will not develop all these plans alone. You will facilitate the collaborative development of a plan that clearly articulates objectives and strategies for implementing a campus vision. First, the vision is developed and articulated. Next, specific objectives and strategies are developed, articulated, and implemented to see to it that the vision is attained. It does us no good to have a vision if no one knows how to make it a reality. The objectives and strategies are the road map to guide the school in vision attainment. They are the plan.

- *Align financial, human, and material resources to support implementation of a campus vision.*

The concept of alignment comes up over and over throughout the competencies. Make sure you clearly understand what it means. In simple terms, it means everything lines up or matches. If you say you need $5,000, six teachers, a paraprofessional, and specific new curriculum to reach a certain goal, then you had better make sure that every single bit of that is clearly defined and allocated in your campus budget. If you do not, then your goals are not aligned with your budget. How can your campus be expected to reach its goals if it does not have the resources necessary to implement the objectives and strategies? For that reason, you must align the financial, human, and material resources necessary to support implementation of the campus vision.

Resources necessary to attain the vision must be in the budget. Resources in the budget must help the campus attain the vision.

- *Establish procedures to assess and modify implementation plans to ensure achievement of the campus vision.*

Having a plan and working the plan are not enough. You must establish procedures to assess and modify implementation plans to ensure achievement of the campus vision. We already know the competencies are serious about the word *ensure*. It does not provide any leeway or excuses. We also know we will have strategies and objectives to guide us toward fulfillment of the campus vision.

All this is important, but it isn't enough. You must also establish procedures to assess and modify the implementation plans in case they are not working perfectly. The word *continuously* is important on TExES. You must facilitate all members of the school community to be continuously assessing and modifying anything and everything that is working well, not working at all, could be working better, or needs to be dumped. Continuously means all the time, without ceasing, even when you are tired, till you die. We once had a pastor who said the seven last words of a dying church are, "We never did it that way before." This is true in all organizations, and especially of schools.

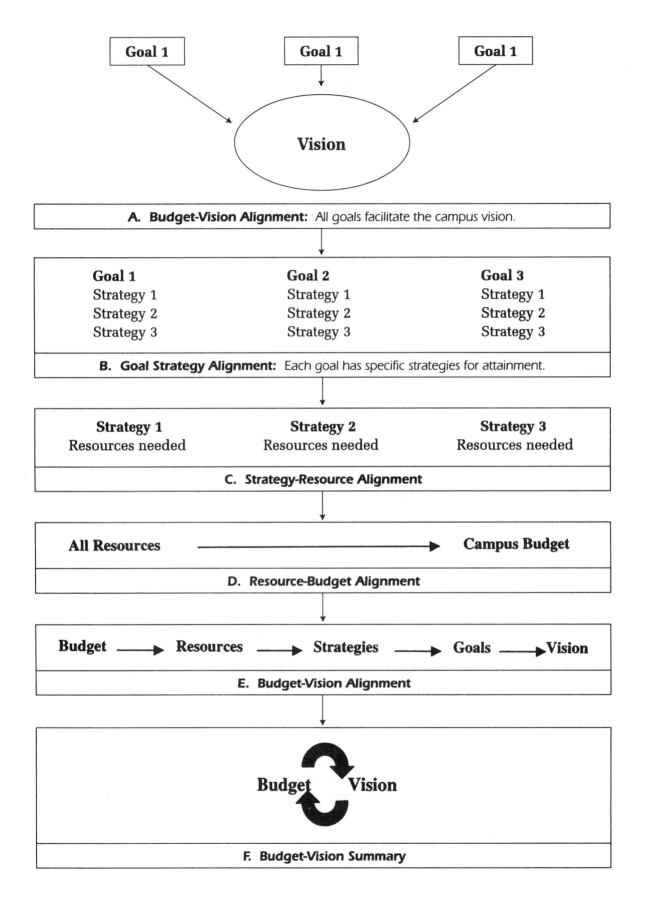

We cannot hang on to old ways of doing things just because it is the way they have always been done. Assess and modify everything! There are no sacred cows, things that cannot be touched. Long-term practices have taken us to the place where too many students are lost between the cracks. It is time to continuously assess and modify implementation plans to ensure achievement of the campus vision.

- *Support innovative thinking and risk taking within the school community and view unsuccessful experiences as learning opportunities.*

This one is pure poetry. Pure poetry! It is just buzzing with beautiful language. Learn to watch for the type of language displayed here because you will see it embedded in words and concepts throughout TExES. Let's see what's so great about this one.

Support innovative thinking and risk taking within the school community. . . Every word of that is terrific! Of course you support innovative thinking and risk taking! What are you supposed to do? Support noninnovative thinking and encourage your staff to stay "in the box" because it is nice, warm, and comfortable in there? No way! We want out of the box so we can respond appropriately to diverse needs in shaping the campus culture. How can we do that unless we are supporting innovative thinking and risk taking? Climb out of that status quo box! There's a whole new world out there!

To view unsuccessful experiences as learning opportunities not only supports innovative thinking and risk taking, it also underlies the entire philosophy of learner-centered leadership. If we really mean it when we say we want to encourage all people to think differently, then they will be entering uncharted ground. When we are doing creative and innovative things and taking risks, of course we will make mistakes. What toddler suddenly one day says, "Gee, I've had enough of this crawling business. I think I will enter the Boston Marathon tomorrow." Of course not! Babies must *learn* how to walk and then run. They pull themselves up, attempt a step or two, fall down, cry, get love from every decent adult around them, then they get up and try again. Eventually, they walk, run, climb trees, and one day graduate from high school, making their parents wish they were toddlers again.

The same is true for teachers and other would be risk takers. While climbing out of the box, they will make mistakes. We cannot expect them to be perfect when they try out new ideas. This is how you handle those mistakes that will determine the climate and valued culture of your campus. If you fuss at them, being tyrannical and dictatorial, chances are they will never offer another innovative idea but stay nice and snug in their own little box, in their own classroom, and never venture out into the scary world of innovation again. They have already tried it, and it wasn't much fun. Getting yelled at or criticized was certainly not a fulfilling professional experience.

But there is a better way. You will be a principal that will view unsuccessful experiences as learning opportunities. We fall down. We get up. It is that simple. Anyone trying something new will eventually fall down. It is inevitable. How we handle the fall is the determining factor in the nurturance and stewardship of the vision. It will determine your leadership style. It will also determine whether others think your walk matches your talk in support of innovative thinking and risk taking. Support your people in both word and deed so they will have the courage to crawl gingerly out on a limb to join you. Success reaps success. Failure reaps failure. Turn unsuccessful experiences into learning opportunities for all. The benefits will be unbelievable.

- *Acknowledge and celebrate the contributions of students, staff members, parents, and community members toward realization of the campus vision.*

If there is one thing we do not do enough of, it's to acknowledge and celebrate the contributions of students, staff members, parents, and community members toward realization of the campus vision. In truth, we are pretty pitiful at it. Kenneth Blanchard and Spencer Johnson in their classic *The One Minute Manager* (1981), as well as Connie Podesta in her *Self-Esteem and the 6-Second Secret* (2001), wrote about how we tend to spend too much time and emphasis on what people do wrong and not nearly enough on clear, specific feedback on what they did right or how they can do something better. We need to praise people more. We need to acknowledge and celebrate all our successes with every human involved. We should share the joy far and wide. Famous college football coach Paul "Bear" Bryant used to say that when his teams did poorly, he took the blame. But when they did well, he gave them the credit. In both cases, the truth was probably a combination of each, yet his success as a coach was largely based on a philosophy of leadership that built others up even if it meant he shouldered undeserved blame.

The same should be true in our schools. We are family. We need to acknowledge and celebrate everything everyone does. If TAAS scores are less than expected, we need to find something good in there to celebrate and to build on for next year. Is the glass half empty or half full? In our schools, they are at least half full all the time. You as principal, as well as every person involved, should be your school's best cheerleader. If you say, "I'm just not the cheerleader type. Besides, that is not my job," I beg to differ. If it is not the job of educators to acknowledge and celebrate contributions and successes of our schools in a free and democratic society, exactly whose job is it?

I rest my case.

Guess My Favorites

Can you guess my favorites? I bet you can! Although I totally support all of them, my two favorites are as follows:

- Support innovative thinking and risk taking within the school community and view unsuccessful experiences as learning opportunities.

- Acknowledge and celebrate the contributions of students, staff members, parents, and community members toward realization of the campus vision.

Important Points To Remember

Watch for answer responses that use these important concepts:

- High expectations are essential to success.
- Collaboration and collegial relationships are fundamental to positive campus culture, climate, and vision.
- Ensure that parents are involved and that appropriate things occur in every aspect of the school community.
- Diversity of persons, thoughts, and deeds are to be encouraged. Innovation begets creativity!
- Triangulation. Use multiple sources of data and factors in decision making.
- Plan, continuously assess, and align everything.
- Support anything that is out of the box. Encourage risk taking.
- Celebrate contributions and successes of everyone and the campus as a whole, no matter how small or large.

Learner-Centered Communication and Community Relations

Domain I: School Community Leadership

Domain Key Concepts: Culture, Climate, Vision

Competency 002

The principal knows how to communicate and collaborate with all members of the school community, respond to diverse interests and needs, and mobilize resources to promote student success.

Communication and collaboration are important leadership concepts in every organization. They are particularly important in schools, where having everyone play a part in developing, articulating, and implementing plans, ideas, and concepts is essential to innovation and future student success. Competency 002 thus focuses on the role of communication and *collaboration* with *all members of the school community*. It does not say to communicate and collaborate only with the members who you like, who will agree with everything you say, or who are leaders in the school community. It says *all* members. That means we must communicate and collaborate even with people who may not be our favorites, as well as those whose goal in life appears to be to cause trouble at the school. Be nice. Solicit their input. Be objective. What can be identified as useful from the input from all sources? Find something of value in every situation. Girl Scouts are taught to always leave a place better than they found it. Should not the same thing be said of educators?

This competency instructs principals to *respond to diverse interests and needs*. Everyone will not have the same interests or needs. Just as there are 31 flavors of ice cream at Baskin-Robbins, there are as many different interests and needs in schools as there are people involved. This goes beyond race, gender, and socioeconomics. It delves into specific individual needs that all humans have. Abraham Maslow's hierarchy of needs[1] goes from lower-level needs of the basics, such as food, clothing, and shelter, to higher-level needs, such as self-confidence, self-awareness, and self-actualization. It may be unrealistic to think we can individualize to the point that all members of the school community will have all their needs met, but the goal of this competency is to try to meet them. Classes do not look the same, act the same, or learn the same way they did in "the good old days." Those days are not coming back—nor should they. Our role is to do everything in our power to respond to the diverse interests and needs of our modern classrooms.

The last component in competency 002 is *mobilizing resources to promote student success*. This means somebody has got to be in charge of getting things together, supplying resources, keeping things organized, and facilitating student success. In this case, that someone is you—the principal. It is your job to mobilize everything necessary to guarantee student growth and productivity. Notice that *mobilize* and *respond* are strong, active verbs. They are not "wimpy" verbs. They are substantive. The competencies do not use wimpy verbs. We do not need wimpy verbs because we do not need wimpy principals. We need strong, proactive, reflective principals who focus on having a positive school culture and climate that focuses exclusively on the specific vision of the school. Now, let's see some ways that principals can accomplish this goal.

The Principal Knows How To . . .

- *Communicate effectively with families and other community members in varied educational contexts.*

The principal must know how to communicate effectively with families and other community members in varied educational contexts. It also goes deeper than that. In addition to knowing how, the principal must actually do it. There is a big difference between knowing how to do something and actually doing it. There are rude people all over the place who know how to be nice—they simply choose not to be. As a positive, proactive, change-oriented principal, you must know how to communicate effectively and actually do it.

Effectively is the key word here. If families and other community members do not understand what you are saying, writing, or otherwise communicating, then you are not communicating effectively. Be aware of this. It is not their job to be better listeners. It is your job to be a better communicator. There may be various reasons why your message is not being understood. The culture and climate of the school may not be aligned with that of the school community. Language or attitudes may be issues. The solution to the communication problem will take analysis and input from families and other community members in varied educational contexts. In other words, you

---

[1] For more information on Maslow's hierarchy, see Maslow, A. H. (1970). Motivation and personality. New York: Harper & Row.

must swallow your pride and go to the source. Talk to the people most closely affected. Solicit input. It is difficult to sell the vision of your school if no one understands what you're saying.

- *Apply skills for building consensus and managing conflict.*

Conflict is an interesting thing. Some people never want any conflict. To have conflict means that people are not agreeing. If people are not agreeing, that means there's diversity of opinion. Hello! Are we not looking for diversity of opinion? If we do not get different views from various people, we'll end up in the muck of status quo–ism, which is exactly where we do not want to be.

On the other hand, we definitely do not want people yelling, screaming, pouting, or getting their feelings hurt because they don't feel their opinions are valued or respected. There has to be a middle ground.

That is why applying skills for building consensus and managing conflict are important. There must be divergent opinions to challenge our perceptions and expectations. These opinions should be actively solicited, listened to, and shared. After thorough, respectful consideration of multiple suggestions and beliefs, a common middle ground must be identified. Through skills for building consensus and managing conflict, the principal kneads all of this together, much as a baker kneads dough. If the bread is not kneaded consistently and with great effort over a long period of time, it won't rise. For the school to experience great expectations, stakeholders will have to be taught skills in listening, mutual respect, and problem solving. Finally, once a decision has been made, everyone must support it. That's part of being a team. Decision making is not an individual effort—it's a group effort and a consensus. The principal must therefore be skilled in group processes to facilitate this end.

- *Implement effective strategies for systematically communicating with and gathering input from all campus stakeholders.*

To facilitate these group processes and team building, the principal must implement effective strategies for systematically communicating with and gathering input from all campus stakeholders. Notice that it does not say to gather input only from campus stakeholders who will agree with you. This is another example of how the competencies reach out to divergent opinions from all stakeholders. Remember, the most important three-letter word in the competencies and on the test is *all*. Watch for it in responses. As it says here, there must be a system for communicating with and gathering input from everyone. It does not happen by chance or good intention. There must be a system. If there is a system, there must be a plan that has been developed. Guess how . . . *collaboratively.* Do everything collaboratively. It is a key to success in learner-centered schools and in passing the TExES.

- *Develop and implement strategies for effective internal and external communications.*

Here are two important concepts. The first is develop and implement strategies. By now you may be sick of hearing about all this developing and implementing of virtually everything. Be sick of it later. Right now, take it to heart. You are the facilitator who sees that all this development and implementation occurs. In this case, you are facilitating strategies for effective internal and external communication.

This brings us to the second point of effective internal and external communications. There is overlap here with the previous discussion of *effective*. If something isn't working, how can it be effective? In using the words *internal* and *external* the competency is trying to make sure you understand that effective communication is not limited to inside the school. You must communicate effectively with all stakeholders, which also includes those external to the school. Families, neighbors, and businesses and churches in the community must understand and support the vision of the school. This cannot occur without strategies for effective internal and external communication. Circulating newsletters, meeting with community groups, visiting places and people outside the school, contacting the media, and using other collaboratively developed strategies to communicate effectively are essential to getting out the message of your vision both inside and outside the school.

- *Develop and implement a comprehensive program of community relations that effectively involves and informs multiple constituencies, including the media.*

Here we go with *develop* and *implement* again. This time, it is in relation to a comprehensive program of community relations that effectively involves and informs multiple constituencies, including the media. Let's take this one by small increments because there is a lot in it.

First, you develop and implement—collaboratively, of course—your plan. This time, the plan is a comprehensive program of community relations. You do this by involving multiple constituencies from varied contexts. This means you involve many different people from diverse places and backgrounds to help develop the plan. Within this charge is the repetition of *effectively*. It does not do any good to develop a plan, or a comprehensive program, of community relations if it is not effective. Community relations includes, among other things, the way the community will perceive or view the school. Obviously, you want the entire community to view the school well, to support its vision by supporting its curriculum, instructional techniques, programs, and culture. You want the community to be *for* the school, never *against* it. Public sentiment has been known to hang by a thread and to change without warning. That is why it's important that your comprehensive program actually be *comprehensive* by involving lots of people (i.e., multiple constituencies), including the media.

Use the media to your advantage. If your district does not have a public relations specialist who coordinates or speaks for the district, be careful of what you say to the media. Usually, less is best because the media sometimes have an uncanny way of misquoting you, even if you give your statement to them in writing. A savvy and wise city manager once told his staff to be careful about picking a fight with anyone who buys ink by the barrel. Educators, too, must heed this advice. Specifically solicit good working relationships with the media. There could be times when you really need their support. And always be careful of everything you say because it may come back in a printed version that isn't exactly what you had in mind.

- *Provide varied and meaningful opportunities for parents/caregivers to be engaged in the education of their children.*

Varied and meaningful opportunities is an important concept. The ideal principal provides an open door and a warm, welcoming climate within and outside of the building. After all, the school belongs to the community, not to its employees. Parents and caregivers, whoever the caregivers may be, deserve to be engaged in the education of their children. Unfortunately, today we have way too many caregivers whom we cannot seem to get involved even when we desperately want their input. This does not mean we can give up. We never give up on anything or anyone. We just keep trying, consistently, day after day, hoping persistence will pay off. You never know what seeds you plant today will reap unknown benefits in the future. So, just keep trying. Never give up.

- *Establish partnerships with parents and caregivers, businesses, and others in the community to strengthen programs and support campus goals.*

Establishing partnerships with virtually everyone is a big deal. This is what collaboration and collegiality is all about. When we establish partnerships everyone becomes invested in the relationship and its outcomes. That is what we want. We want everyone engaged in strengthening programs and supporting campus goals. We want everyone in a partnership with us, never against us. If there is anyone against us, they are the first with whom we want to work on developing relationships and partnerships. This includes parents and caregivers, businesses, and others—everyone in the school community. Watch for responses that address strong collaboration and partnerships with others outside the campus.

- *Communicate and work effectively with diverse groups in the school community to ensure that all students have an equal opportunity for educational success.*

Have you noticed that there are specific competency words and concepts that repeat themselves over and over? Pay attention to them. If they were not important, they would not keep coming up. This time, we are again looking at communicating and working effectively with diverse groups in the school community. This is important because even though the concept of working with community members in varied educational contexts and all stakeholders has been brought up repeatedly and both of those include diverse groups, this is such an important issue that they spell it out for you. They do not want you to take any chances of missing the point that *working effectively with diverse groups* is paramount to success. It is a classic example of the teaching strategy of "Tell them. Tell them again with different language. Tell them one more time in still another way. Then, in closing, tell them what they just learned." The competencies want to make sure you know that working effectively with diverse groups is very, very important. Remember that as you lead your school. Remember it while taking the TExES and looking at various answers. Look for the answers in which the concept of soliciting input from lots of people of varied backgrounds and experiences is stressed. That's usually the correct answer. Without the total support of diverse groups in the school community, how can you ensure (did you catch that verb?) that all students have an equal opportunity for educational success?

I must elaborate on all students having an equal opportunity for educational success. It may be true in the United States that all people are created equal, but when it comes to education, that's quite a stretch. Every student comes with different experiences and with different baggage. Some arrive at school hungry. Consider Maslow's work. How can anyone concentrate on learning if they're hungry? Hunger is just the tip of the iceberg when it comes to student differences. Can we solve all the social problems of the world? Regretfully, no. We can do everything possible to facilitate every student at our own schools in having, at minimum, an equal opportunity for educational success by attempting to meet their educational and individual needs. Too many of our students do not have anyone who really cares about them. At the Ideal School, at least they will have us. If our teachers cannot buy into this philosophy of helping students on all levels, to provide them with an equal opportunity, then guess what? It's time for them to look for a new career.

- *Respond to pertinent political, social, and economic issues in the internal and external environment.*

This concept asks that you keep your eyes open. Be aware of what is going on in the world. Don't let yourself get so caught up in what's going on inside the school that you lose track of what's going on outside the school. This even goes beyond the school community. It involves pertinent political, social, and economic issues around the world. No man is an island, and no school is an island, either. We cannot operate in isolation. Everything going on in the world—and particularly in our communities—has an impact on schools. Be cognizant of local, state, national, and world affairs. Encourage your faculty, staff, and the students to stay up with current events. It is the systems approach to life. Everything is connected. Nothing happens in isolation.

Guess My Favorite

Have you guessed my favorite? It's the following:

- Communicate and work effectively with diverse groups in the school community to ensure that all students have an equal opportunity for educational success.

There's pure poetry in that one—don't miss it. Why are we here if not to ensure that all students have an equal opportunity for educational success? It's what we're all about as educators. If you do not believe in this one, quit now. Education is not for you.

Important Points to Remember

- Work and communicate effectively with everyone—both inside and outside the school.
- Encourage discussion and input from people with different opinions while nurturing consensus and managing conflict.
- Community relations can make you or break you. Nurture them!
- Engage parents, caregivers, businesses, and everyone else, including strangers on the street, in partnerships and meaningful opportunities to be a part of the school family.
- Keep your eyes open to respond to everything taking place in the world that could impact students or education.
- Ensure that all students have an equal opportunity for success in every facet of their lives.

Learner-Centered Values and Ethics of Leadership

Domain I: School Community Leadership

Domain Key Concepts: Culture, Climate, Vision

Competency 003

The principal knows how to act with integrity, fairness, and in an ethical and legal manner.

In its simplest form, this competency says the principal should do what is morally right at all times, even if it is not politically correct. This is the classic place to make sure your walk matches your talk. It is one thing to say that all people should be treated with integrity, fairness, and in an ethical and legal manner, but it is something else entirely to practice this ideal. Often, this can be a classic case of "Do as I say, not as I do."

Although all of this may sound easy, we know that it really isn't. The Cadet Prayer at West Point asks God for guidance in doing the "harder right versus the easier wrong." Competency 003 expects educators to do the same thing.

The Principal Knows How To . . .

- *Model and promote the highest standard of conduct, ethical principles, and integrity in decision-making, actions, and behaviors.*

It is one thing to promote the highest standard of conduct, ethical principles, and integrity in decision-making, actions, and behaviors. It is an entirely different matter to *model* the same behavior. It's a lot easier said than done, even for those who want to do right. Do not write off this competency as an easy thing to do. It may be the most difficult of all.

- *Implement policies and procedures that promote professional educator compliance with the* Code of Ethics and Standard Practices for Texas Educators.

The Code of Ethics and Standard Practices for Texas Educators is basically a common sense document of ethical behaviors. You do not need to memorize it. Review it before the test, but don't dwell on it. If you aren't yet familiar with this document, it is available on the Internet: www.texes.nesinc.com/texesstudyguid/. Click on "Professional Development" and then the "Code of Ethics and Standard Practices for Texas Educators." Review it to make sure you synthesize its concepts.

- *Apply knowledge of ethical issues affecting education.*

Knowing the ethical thing to do is different from applying it. Make sure you are a model of ethical behavior inside and outside of school. As an administrator, your life is a fishbowl. An entire school community is watching everything you do.

- *Apply legal guidelines (e.g., in relation to students with disabilities, bilingual education, confidentiality, discrimination) to protect the rights of students and staff members and to improve learning opportunities.*

Two vital responsibilities of any principal are to protect the rights of students and staff members and to improve learning opportunities. It shouldn't be necessary to be reminded of legal guidelines. Individual educational plans (IEPs) provide a good example of the need to apply legal guidelines. If a student with a disability moves to your school and his IEP says he should jump rope backward in the shade of a west-facing tree at 10:01 every morning, you had better make sure he does just that until another ARD (admission, review, and/or dismissal meeting) can be held to modify his care plan. Until then, it is the law.

Various examples of legal guidelines regarding students with disabilities, bilingual education, confidentiality, and discrimination are provided in the competency that address concerns within the school community. An easier way to remember which guidelines to apply is to consistently apply them all. If it is the law or a policy, do it. If you truly hate it, contact your legislator or other policymaker to discuss why you hate it and why you think it should be changed.

- *Apply laws, policies, and procedures in a fair and reasonable manner.*

Be consistent. Apply laws, policies, and procedures in a fair and reasonable manner for all people. Do not play favorites. If something could be construed as unethical, immoral, or illegal behavior, don't do it. Do not set yourself up for criticism. Apply rules consistently and fairly.

- *Articulate the importance of education in a free democratic society.*

To articulate is to put voice to the importance of education. It is the role of all educators, not just administrators, to articulate the importance of education in a free democratic society. If it's not our responsibility, then whose is it? It's been said that today's school administrators are so busy with management duties, there's little time left for the role of statesperson that educators traditionally have played. We cannot let this responsibility slip away. It is one we carry with us at school, at home, at church, in the community, and in everything we do.

- *Serve as an advocate for all children.*

Again, if advocating for children is not the responsibility of educators, particularly educators in the public schools, then whose is it? I take this responsibility very seriously and want you to do so as well. Our children are our future, our legacy. We cannot write off a single child. To care is not enough; to advocate for children requires action. It means not being afraid to speak up for the oppressed, the downtrodden, the sick, the disabled, or the hungry. It means standing up for those who do not speak English, who have no money, or who struggle with abuse or neglect. It means giving every student a second—or a hundredth—chance to get an education and, to the best of our ability, removing obstacles to their success.

Being an advocate is an emotionally draining experience. You should know that going in. There will be times when you think you just cannot do this anymore. You are tired, frustrated, and just plain spent. When those times occur, take a day or two away from school. Do not feel guilty. You need this time of respite and retreat to recharge physically, emotionally, and spiritually. Take it, and don't look back. Don't answer the phone. Let your soul have the quiet time it needs to rest, reflect, and regain strength away from the busyness, craziness, and stresses of your life. You will be a better person and a better administrator when you return. If you are going to be an advocate for all children, there are times when you'll feel drained of all energy. But the effort is worth it if you really believe in a free democratic society. The future of that society is our children. They are our future. They are our responsibility.

- *Promote the continuous and appropriate development of all students.*

The key words here are *continuous* and *appropriate*. Students are going to develop regardless. They may or may not develop in appropriate ways. It is the responsibility of the principal, as well as all of society, to see to it that all students have continuous and appropriate development. *Continuous* means all the time, without ceasing. It means you can never give up on seeking to mentor and guide the development of every student with whom you have contact. It is not limited to academic development, but to every facet of student maturation. For those who think they did not enter education to take on raising every single child, there is one thing to remember. The role of educators is to nurture every student continuously.

- *Promote awareness of learning differences, multicultural awareness, gender sensitivity, and ethnic appreciation.*

All people, whether they are 3 years old or 50 years old, learn differently. This isn't news, yet for many classrooms in the United States, teachers act as if they don't know this. They continue to "stand and deliver" instruction that often is not one bit meaningful to the experiences, culture, gender, or ethnicity of students who are held captive in the classroom, sitting there not really listening or caring. And then we wonder about the future of education.

If we know students have different learning styles and modalities, that they come with different experiences, genders, and cultures, why are we treating them as if we thought everyone of them were alike? As positive, proactive, student-centered school leaders, it is imperative that you promote awareness of learning differences, multicultural awareness, gender sensitivity, and ethnic and religious appreciation. Promoting it by articulation only is not enough. You must be in there proactively, role modeling the type of leadership you expect teachers and others to display in classrooms and in the community. Furthermore, you must reward appropriate behavior from your staff. Praise them. Nurture a vision for the school that includes and appreciates every student, teacher, and community member regardless of their differences.

Guess My Favorites

It is virtually impossible for me to pick a single favorite in this competency. In fact, I have more favorites in 003 than in all the others, which is saying a lot. Here they are, as if you hadn't guessed:

- Articulate the importance of education in a free democratic society.
- Serve as an advocate for all children.
- Promote the continuous and appropriate development of all students.
- Promote awareness of learning differences, multicultural awareness, gender sensitivity, and ethnic appreciation.

Important Points to Remember

- Treat every student as if the future of our country depended on how this single human being is nurtured and developed.
- Let your walk match your talk in every facet of your life. This includes your private life as well as your professional life.
- Be ethical, moral, consistent, fair, and legal at all times.
- Students are human beings. They come from different circumstances. Do not try to make them all the same. Do not try to make them into

something they are not. Value, cherish, and appreciate their individual cultures, ethnic backgrounds, genders, circumstances, and experiences. Treat every one of them as if they were your own or as if they were the very student who will grow up and marry your child or grandchild. Think about it. Act accordingly.

- One more thing. Be an advocate for all children!

Learner-Centered Curriculum Planning and Development

Domain II: Instructional Leadership

Domain Key Concepts: Curriculum, Instruction, Staff Development

Competency 004

The principal knows how to facilitate the design and implementation of curricula and strategic plans that enhance teaching and learning; ensure alignment of curriculum, instruction, resources, and assessment; and promote the use of varied assessments to measure student performance.

Remember that while reviewing Competency 001, we discussed the progression of development, articulation, implementation, and stewardship of the vision of the school? The same process is used in Competency 004 as the principal facilitates the design and implementation of curricula and strategic plans that enhance teaching and learning. Notice it says the principal *facilitates* this design. It does not say the principal does it alone.

On the TExES examination, be careful to watch for answers that sound excellent but discuss responsibilities that are not the principal's. The test developers include these to determine whether you are collaborative in your leadership style and whether you delegate and empower others to further their professional growth. An example of this is the principal's facilitating the design and implementation of curricula and strategic plans. By facilitating, the principal supplies needed resources, including time and support, to teachers and others involved in decision making such that appropriate curricula and strategic plans will occur.

Strategic planning for curriculum and instruction, as well as for every other school venture, is critically important to teaching and learning. First, identification of campus strengths and weaknesses must occur. This is followed by systematically analyzing how strengths can be used to support and develop weaknesses. There must be a plan to address every type of weakness. Without one, you'll simply wander through the wilderness of school administration, hoping student learning will be enhanced somehow. But you'll never be sure it is, because no systematic plan exists to identify goals and strategies for implementation and no tools for assessment are in place. The systematic plan provides a basic framework within which every stakeholder in the learning community is working and focused. There must always be a systematic campus improvement plan through which the following tasks are achieved:

- Collaborative identification of campus, grade, or subject goals
- Detailing and implementation of strategies and techniques, including technology use, to attain these goals
- Definition of timelines to be used as benchmarks to measure progress
- Formative and summative assessment to determine if progress has been made
- Continuous modification to enhance the productivity of the plan as measured by increased student learning and progress toward the campus vision

Notice that the key terms of *design* and *implementation* are used repeatedly within the competencies. Watch for those words, or others that mean the same thing, on the test. These are important roles of the principal. They will be embedded in TExES questions and responses.

The competency goes on to focus on the role of the principal to ensure alignment of curriculum, instruction, resources, and assessment. The issue of alignment appears repeatedly in the competencies (see Figure 3.1). It is obviously one of the test designers' favorites. In this case, it relates to curriculum, instruction, resources, and assessment. But what does it mean?

Very simply, it means this: Do these factors—curriculum, instruction, resources, and assessment—work together? A curriculum is *what* is taught. Instruction is *how* it is taught. Resources are the tools used in the instruction of curricula. Assessment, of course, is measurement of the first three factors. Ideally, each of these factors is connected. Appropriate instructional strategies are aligned with what is taught. Appropriate resources to accomplish this goal are budgeted and provided for. Then, the results of these endeavors are tested or alternatively measured. All of this should be documented in the campus plan, lesson plans, and the budget. If any piece is missing, the system will not work efficiently. The result will be a lack of appropriate teaching and learning.

Few educators think they are not testing what is taught at their schools. The only true way to know, however, is through a thorough needs assessment and curriculum alignment. These are major, time-consuming projects if they are done right. And if they are not done right, they are not worth doing at all. That means they are not something you can accomplish at Tuesday afternoon's faculty meeting. It will take longer than that just to figure out what needs to be done and how to do it. Needs assessments and curriculum alignments should be well thought out and systematically planned with significant input from the entire learning community. All these data go into the development and refinement of campus goals and progress toward the campus vision.

Sometimes surprising things are revealed. Although teachers may think they are spending significant amounts of time teaching a specific concept, the curriculum alignment could reveal that they aren't. It should come as no surprise when analysis of test data reveals student weaknesses in the same area. The same can be true conversely. Sometimes too much time is spent on a concept students have mastered, and it's time to move on.

Needs assessments and curricula alignments should occur at the district as well as the campus level. Data analysis is exceedingly important. It is the foundation on which sound curricular and instructional decisions can be made. It allows us to ensure, not simply to hope, that our schools will improve. Ensuring, not hoping, is what our quest toward the campus vision demands. Anything less is a waste of time.

The ideal principal promotes the use of varied assessments to measure student performance. That means that, contrary to popular belief, the Texas Assessment of Academic Skills is not the "be all and end all" of student assessment. It is one tool, although a very important one in Texas, by which we assess our students. But there are many other, alternative forms of assessment available that should also be used. Successful schools often use a constructivist approach to teaching. Authentic assessment through student demonstrations of learning as well as performance and project development are also used. We must capitalize on the use of multiple intelligences, multisensory, and other forms of assessment that address individual learning styles. Are standardized forms of assessment important? Of course. But there are also many students, including adult learners, who for various reasons simply do not do well on standardized or other forms of paper-and-pencil tests. This doesn't mean they aren't intelligent or that they aren't learning. It means their learning must be measured by varied assessments. In the ideal school, led by the ideal principal, varied assessments are used to measure student performance.

The Principal Knows How To . . .

- *Facilitate effective campus curriculum planning based on knowledge of various factors (e.g., emerging issues, occupational and economic trends, demographic data, student learning data, motivation theory, teaching and learning theory, principles of curriculum design, human developmental processes, legal requirements).*

The principal is the instructional leader of the school. To be the instructional leader, the principal must facilitate campus curriculum planning based on knowledge of various factors. These factors include, but are not limited to, emerging issues, occupational and economic trends, demographic data, student learning data, motivation theory, teaching and learning theory, principles of curriculum design, human developmental processes, and legal requirements. By analyzing these various factors, you are using triangulation, as discussed in Chapter 3; that is, you will facilitate curriculum planning. You do not have to be an expert on every issue. You will empower others as you collaboratively integrate curricular planning for school improvement.

- *Facilitate the use of sound, research-based practice in the development, implementation, and evaluation of campus curricular, cocurricular, and extracurricular programs.*

We've returned to the development, implementation, and evaluation theme. You can see how this progression of steps is used over and over again in the competencies. This time, it is in reference to the use of sound, research-based practice . . . of campus curricular, cocurricular, and extracurricular programs. You could substitute the word *all* for the words *curricular, cocurricular,* and *extracurricular* programs. The idea is that sound, research-based practice is developed, implemented, and evaluated.

Your own ongoing professional development is important. Just because you complete your preparation program and certification requirements does not mean that you can stop learning. You must continue to read, study, attend professional conferences, participate in discussions, and conduct action research to stay current. Do not make the mistake of planning professional development activities for your staff and none for yourself. You also need— and deserve—to grow. Your campus staff needs to see that you value development enough to participate in growth activities and not just tell them to do it. They will see you walk the walk, and this will stimulate their professional growth. Your collective growth will have positive benefits to teaching and learning at your school.

- *Facilitate campus participation in collaborative district planning, implementation, monitoring and revision of curriculum to ensure appropriate scope, sequence, content, and alignment.*

By now you are recognizing the common pattern of planning (or developing), implementing, monitoring, and revising (or modifying) of virtually everything. This time, it is in reference to curriculum, ensuring (did you catch *ensure*?) appropriate scope, sequence, content, and alignment.

Alignment, by now, is our good friend. We know what that means. It means to match up everything appropriately to make sure it is doing what it is supposed to do. Scope and sequence are the big and little pictures of curriculum planning. Scope is where you are going. Sequence is the path to get you there. Think of it as a Covey[1] "begin-with-the-end-in-mind" concept with the scope of the curriculum content the end you have in mind.

---

[1] See Covey, S. R. (1990). *The seven habits of highly effective people.* New York: Simon & Schuster.

Bringing all this together, the principal is the facilitator of campus participation in collaborative (sound familiar?) district planning. Notice that this time the principal is working with the district in addition to the campus itself for district planning, implementation, monitoring, and revision of curriculum. Last, the principal is ensuring that appropriate (not just what comes next in the textbook) scope, sequence, content, and alignment occur. This is a very heavy responsibility.

- *Facilitate the use of appropriate assessments to measure student learning and ensure educational accountability.*

Appropriate is another word to watch for. It comes up over and over. This time, it is in relation to assessment. There are all kinds of assessments. Different ones may have different values for different situations. No specific form of assessment is perfect for every student or situation. Different topics as well as different student learning styles and modalities require different forms of assessment. That is the point the test designers try to make with the phrase *appropriate assessments to measure student learning and ensure* (ensure, again) *educational accountability.* The assessment must be appropriate, or there will not be true accountability. Think of it as a validity and reliability comparison. If the assessment is not appropriate, there can be no true educational accountability.

- *Facilitate the use of technology, telecommunications, and information systems to enrich the campus curriculum.*

Domain III discusses technology and information systems in relation to the management of the school. In this component, technology, telecommunications, and information systems are tools to be used to enrich the campus curriculum. Domain II focuses on curriculum, instruction, and staff development, so the technology issues here are curriculum and instruction related. It is the role of the principal to facilitate the use of all forms of technology within the curriculum appropriately.

- *Facilitate the effective coordination of campus curricular, cocurricular, and extracurricular programs in relation to other district programs.*

The principal is the person responsible for tying all the different programs and facets of the school together, making sure they are aligned and not in conflict, and ensuring that everything runs properly and in congruence with the campus vision. As such, you must facilitate the effective coordination of campus curricular, cocurricular, and extracurricular programs in relation to other district programs. Notice that it does not say you have to do all this single-handedly, and you won't unless your goal is sheer exhaustion. You are to facilitate these programs and activities not just in relation to your campus, but in relation to other district programs as well. As facilitator and coordinator, you are the liaison for making sure all these things run smoothly and in conjunction with campus goals and priorities.

- *Promote the use of creative thinking, critical thinking, and problem solving by staff members and other campus stakeholders involved in curriculum design and delivery.*

This is an important point. It is directed toward the heart of curricular and instructional issues. The principal must promote the use of creative thinking, critical thinking, and problem solving. Is that not the purpose of education? Should not all curriculum and instructional techniques be geared toward the development of *creative thinking, critical thinking, and problem solving* from students and from the entire learning community? This should be one of our most primary goals and a definite focus of our campus vision. If it is not, we have missed a significant purpose in our existence.

It goes on to say that campus stakeholders involved in curriculum design and delivery should participate in this creative and critical thinking and problem solving. Is that not what we just said? Are we not brilliant? Next time *we* can develop TExES. What do you think? We could exercise some creative and critical thinking to problem solve the situation.

Guess My Favorite

I know this is going to come as a big surprise, but my favorite is:

- Promote the use of creative thinking, critical thinking, and problem solving by staff and other campus stakeholders involved in curriculum design and delivery.

Important Points to Remember

- Facilitate everything. Dictate nothing.
- Triangulate everything by looking at various forms of data to make informed decisions.
- Empower others but ensure things happen that are supposed to happen.
- Ensure that curriculum, instruction, technology, and assessment are appropriate.
- Make sure all campus and district programs are coordinated appropriately.
- Promote, stress, facilitate, and ensure that everyone involved in the school community is using creative and critical thinking to facilitate problem solving in all areas.

Learner-Centered Instructional Leadership and Management

Domain II: Instructional Leadership

Domain Key Concepts: Curriculum, Instruction, Staff Development

Competency 005

The principal knows how to advocate, nurture, and sustain an instructional program and a campus culture that are conducive to student learning and staff professional growth.

Remember while reviewing Competency 001 that we discussed facilitating the development, articulation, implementation, and stewardship of a vision? Competency 005 is its sister. This time, instead of focusing on the vision of the school, we are focusing on the instructional program and campus culture, but the idea is the same. Both times the principal must advocate, nurture, and sustain something, whether that something is the campus vision, teacher's instruction, or campus culture, for it to be shared, advocated, nurtured, and sustained.

It is obvious that the principal should advocate virtually anything that is conducive to student learning and staff professional development, but that isn't enough. What if there are principals whose walk does not match their talk? I know that's an amazing concept, but believe it or not, there are some out there. It will not be you. You will go beyond advocating, to nurturing. What is nurturing? Think of parenting. Think of how parents look after, feed, protect, and do everything within their capabilities to make sure their children have everything they need to thrive. Now think of the instructional programs and campus climate as your children. You cannot just leave the school community with a curriculum guide and hope for the best. You have to nourish and protect it, and sometimes you have to wipe away the tears. It's your responsibility to comfort, discipline, and nurture the members of your community because you want them to grow up to be wonderful human beings. You do it because you love them.

The same is true in nurturing your campus. You must nourish, cuddle, and comfort everyone involved in your school community. This includes students, teachers, staff members, and families. You must be the iron hand with the velvet glove when you discipline them. You must wipe their tears when they fall down, and you must celebrate their joys and triumphs. This is how you develop a family. Your school is a family. For too many children, the school may be the closest thing to a family they have. They may act as if they don't care what goes on, but deep inside they do. Teachers and other staff members do, too. You are the shepherd of the flock. Take care of it. That's what nurturing the entire campus means, and it includes student learning and staff professional growth. Encourage staff members in their pursuits toward improving student learning as they seek to enhance their own professional growth. Reward their efforts and celebrate their successes. Your campus is growing up around you. You are the parent. You are nurturing your children. You are feeding your flock. The real rewards are intrinsic as you see increased student and staff learning.

So you have advocated and nurtured this learning climate, but how do you sustain it? This is similar to stewardship of the vision that we discussed in Competency 001. It is far more difficult to sustain anything because once basic goals have been met, there is a basic human tendency to lessen intensity of effort. And when intensity lessens, so does passion and then our commitment to a cause greater than ourselves. If we simply maintain and do not advance, we become the status quo we have worked so hard to change. If we accept the status quo, we soon become stagnant. Anything stagnant soon begins to stink. Who could possibly want a stinking school or principal?

Not us. We want a growing, vibrant, intense, warm, supportive campus. That is why it is imperative that you sustain the focus on current, research-based curriculum, instruction, assessment, and growth for students and staff. Keeping this sustenance constant can be physically, emotionally, and spiritually draining on everyone, including you. Sometimes you have to step back, retreat, and reflect. You have to regroup. Sometimes you may need to take a day off to stay home and let your soul take precedence over your body and mind. The difference between hope and despair is often nothing more than a good night's sleep. It is amazing what that can do.

The same is true for your staff. They work hard, too. There will be times when they need a few minutes or even a day to rest, to regroup, and to get their acts together again. There's no crime in this for you or for them. Does it cost to pay a substitute for a day? Yes, it does. Some schools say they cannot afford it. But the cost of a substitute could be an investment that is well worth it if a teacher comes back refreshed and refocused on helping students become all they can be. The ideal principal works creatively to allow time for staff members to reflect, refocus, and learn. This constitutes a learning community.

The Principal Knows How To . . .

- *Facilitate the development of a campus learning organization that supports instructional improvement and change through ongoing study of relevant research and best practice.*

The principal is the learning leader of the campus. Effective principals participate in many different types of professional growth and development to study relevant research and best practice. They are current and knowledgeable about new strategies and techniques. They share their knowledge with the rest of the school and community, always striving to infuse new ideas on their campuses. They are lifelong learners in the truest sense of the word. They are not reading, researching, attending conferences, visiting other campuses, or participating in discussions with other professionals just because they should. They are doing it because their hearts are in it. They love learning and want to share that love with others. In this case, the others are members of the school community. Because of this nurturance of adult learning, they are continuously trying new ideas that support instructional improvement and change. The idea is never to quit trying to improve, never to quit asking how we can do things better, and never, ever to settle for the status quo.

- *Facilitate the implementation of sound, research-based instructional strategies, decisions, and programs in which multiple opportunities to learn and be successful are available to all students.*

We continue here as you, a wonderful, change-oriented principal, facilitate the implementation of sound, research-based instructional strategies, decisions, and programs. But you don't stop there. You don't want to take any chances of status quo–ism setting in. You are constantly leading the campus to question new ways to help every student, motivated or not, to learn. You sustain a continuous emphasis on quality as defined by students learning and learning well. To do that, campus strategies, decisions, and programs must provide multiple opportunities, not just one or two opportunities, for all students to be successful. Notice it doesn't say that just the students who are motivated or are class officers will be successful. It says *all* students. That means everyone.

- *Create conditions that encourage staff members, students, families/ caregivers, and the community to strive to achieve the campus vision.*

Creating conditions in the learning environment is part of developing a nurturing and supportive campus climate. Long-term effectiveness and productivity are dependent on a good working and learning environment. Encouraging others in positive ways to think outside of the box, to take risks, and to respond to and appreciate diversity of backgrounds and experiences are all examples of nurturing the campus vision. All stakeholders, including staff members, students, families or other caregivers, and the community, must be encouraged and nurtured to work hard, to strive to achieve the campus vision. The campus vision always entails excellence. Excellence is not achieved without taking risks, trying new strategies and programs, implementing new research and best practices; it is not achieved without shared decision making. Together we build. Together we succeed.

- *Ensure that all students are provided high-quality, flexible instructional programs with appropriate resources and services to meet individual student needs.*

Notice that the verb used is *ensure*. To ensure means to guarantee, not to hope, that things will work out. As a truly great principal, one that passes the TExES exam right off the bat, you will ensure, not hope, that every student in your school is provided high-quality, flexible instructional programs. You will be certain your budget is aligned with your campus goals such that appropriate resources and services are available to achieve the vision. Your campus will never settle for the same old ordinary routine of daily practice. Your campus will constantly be trying new things, infusing new programs, experimenting with different techniques, conducting action research, and being vibrant and alive with creative possibilities to meet individual student needs.

There will be teachers and others who do not want to become actively engaged in any part of students' lives except the cognitive aspects. They will feel that it isn't their job or their business to attempt to meet individual student needs. They are wrong. It is part of our role as professional educators to act with integrity and fairness and in an ethical and legal manner as described in Competency 003. Of course, it is more demanding physically and emotionally to attempt to actively engage in meeting individual student needs. These needs go beyond basic academics. There are other facets to students' lives. Nonetheless, there is a fine line between being interested and supportive and being intrusive. Good principals walk that fine line and encourage their staff to walk along with them to support the needs of all students.

- *Use formative and summative student assessment data to develop, support, and improve campus instructional strategies and goals.*

Here is a simple way to keep the terms *formative* and *summative* straight in your mind. The first four letters of formative are "form." When you form something, you take part in its creation from the beginning. Therefore, formative assessment comes at the beginning or near the beginning of planning instruction, programs, needs assessments, community endeavors, and so forth.

On the other hand, the first letters of summative are "sum," as in "summarize." In adding, the sum is the total of the numbers. It is what you get when you are finished and add up everything. The same is true of summative assessment. Summative assessment, similar to summative staff evaluative conferences, comes at the end when you are summarizing a situation. Therefore, by using various data sources for both formative and summative assessment, the campus team can get a better, more global picture of how students are growing, learning, and developing. That is our goal. We want to use many different sources of data, taken at different points to develop, support, and improve campus instructional strategies and goals. If we do not use both formative and summative information, then intelligent, nonbiased, data-driven decision making cannot occur. Without that, why should anyone be surprised when measurable progress toward campus goals is not made? If we do not know where we are, how can we know where we're going and whether we're making progress on the journey? What gets measured gets done. Without continuous formative and summative assessment, progress is only optional. Lack of measurable progress is not an option. We want every child to grow, learn, and succeed. We also want every teacher, paraprofessional, and staff member to grow, learn, and succeed. Therefore, we set goals, we determine how we are going to meet them, and then we use both formative and summative student data to improve everything we do.

- *Facilitate the use and integration of technology, telecommunications, and information systems to enhance learning,*

We are in the fifth of nine competencies. This is the first direct reference to technology. That doesn't mean that technology hasn't been important in other facets of the school, particularly in the development of vision, goals, and instructional strategies. This is why its use must be integrated into all parts of planning, curriculum, instruction, programs, and into the facilities themselves. Ever-changing and expanding technology is here to stay. As principal, you will facilitate the use and integration of technology, telecommunications, and information systems to enhance learning. You will use team collaborative planning as well as formative and summative assessment to determine how this will occur. Information systems will be up-to-date to facilitate the efficient management of data. Telecommunications will be innovative and student centered. Partnerships with businesses, regional service centers, other schools, and universities will be enhanced through networking. As principal, you will facilitate new and innovative ways to integrate the use of technology to enhance learning for everyone, including yourself.

- *Facilitate the implementation of sound, research-based theories and techniques of teaching, learning, classroom management, student discipline, and school safety to ensure a campus environment conducive to teaching and learning.*

An easy way to address this would be to put a parenthesis before the word *teaching* and another parenthesis after *safety*. We could then substitute the word *everything* for *teaching, learning, classroom management, student discipline, and school safety.* Of course, it is the responsibility of the principal to facilitate the implementation of sound, research-based theories and techniques of everything. What are we supposed to do? Use sound, research-based theories for some things and not others? What can we exclude? Nothing. Therefore, you can consider teaching, learning, classroom management, student discipline, and school safety an elaboration of the word everything. The writers of the competencies wanted to elaborate on specific, sound, research-based theories and techniques with examples. All of these—and everything else that takes place in the entire school community—should exist for the single purpose of ensuring a campus environment that is conducive to teaching and learning. This is why we're here. It's our job and our place in society. It's what we do. We use sound, research-based theories and techniques as our tools to enhance teaching and learning and create a better world.

- *Facilitate the development, implementation, evaluation, and refinement of student services and activity programs to fulfill academic, developmental, social, and cultural needs.*

We have seen this process before. In fact, by now we're old friends with facilitating the development, implementation, evaluation, and refinement of virtually everything. We have used it with shared vision, curriculum, instruction, assessment, and staff development. Now we are applying the same process to student services and activity programs.

There are some who erroneously think student services and activity programs, such as climate and culture, are unimportant. They think these are frills and not necessary to student learning. They are wrong. Student services and activity programs help constitute campus climate and culture. They help define who we are, what we value, what we appreciate, what our traditions are, and the subtle nuances that make one school different from another. They are the things that make us unique. We should not try to be any other school. We should seek to develop, nurture, and capitalize on the special things that fulfill the academic, developmental, social, and cultural needs of our school's students and community.

Each school will have its own student services and activity programs. There will be some commonalities among most schools such as football, volleyball, band, and art. But there will be different programs that are successful at one school and less so at another. There is nothing wrong with that. What's important is that each school have the appropriate programs to meet the needs of their students academically, developmentally, socially, and culturally. Work collaboratively with your students, faculty, staff, and community to find new and innovative ways to involve and engage as many people as possible in services and programs that will enhance the vision of the school and community.

- *Analyze instructional needs and allocate resources effectively and equitably.*

When I ran for my first term on our school board, my campaign treasurer went around telling people, "Show me the money!" He knew support without financial contributions was great, but it wouldn't help us fund the campaign. Running any campaign is expensive. I was fortunate to have many friends and supporters to help study and define the issues and community as well as to help solicit the necessary resources. Without the nickels and dimes and grassroots support of citizens from a diversity of backgrounds, I would not have had the financial support necessary to fund my campaign. Thank goodness it paid off!

The same is true inside our schools. We have to study and analyze the instructional needs of students. We know that to make intelligent, informed, nonbiased decisions, we must use many types of data. Therefore, our analysis becomes an issue of, "Show me the data." Without appropriate data, we cannot pinpoint specific instructional needs and allocate resources effectively and equitably.

This is another example of the issue of alignment. The campus vision must be collaboratively developed and articulated. Specific goals that meet instructional needs of students must be determined. All the resources necessary to meet these campus goals must then be included in the school's budget. Conversely, there should be nothing in the budget that is not reflected in the campus goals. When the campus goals and budget match, they are aligned. When something appears in one but not the other, they are not aligned. As we've discussed, the same is true of other aspects of campus administration: Curriculum and assessment must be aligned, as must campus and individual needs and staff professional development. For a campus to be effective, everything must be perfectly aligned (Figure 7.1).

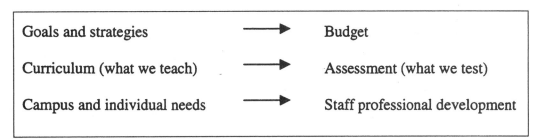

Figure 7.1. For a Campus to Be Effective, Everything Must Be Perfectly Aligned

- *Analyze the implications of various factors (e.g., staffing patterns, class scheduling formats, school organizational structures, student discipline practices) for teaching and learning.*

This is similar to the last time we saw a list of examples. Inside the parentheses, you could substitute the word *everything* again. As part of the advocacy, nurturance, and sustenance of proactive student learning, the principal studies data from myriad sources. Through a collaborative and shared decision-making process, the team analyzes the implications of various factors that affect teaching and learning. These include, but are not limited to, staffing patterns, class scheduling formats, school organizational structures, and student discipline practices. Nothing is left out or exempt. The campus team is continuously observant of changes in the learning environment, ready to respond proactively to potential problems by solving them before they develop. There is nothing worse than to play the "If Only" game. "If only we had done this," or "If only we had done that, such and such would not have occurred and created this big mess!" By analyzing the contextual implications of various factors (societal, family, socioeconomic, language, etc.) of teaching and learning, informed, intelligent, proactive (vs. *reactive*) decision making can occur.

- *Ensure responsiveness to diverse sociological, linguistic, cultural, and other factors that may affect students' development and learning.*

This is a great one. It begins with the strong verb *ensure*. It does not say encourage, solicit, or hope. It says you will ensure responsiveness to diverse sociological, linguistic, cultural, and other factors. That means you must see to it that the school community is responsive to the needs of its students. There are no excuses. The diversity of sociological, linguistic, cultural, and other factors will be addressed. They will not be left to chance or whim. All students and community members will be valued and appreciated for their uniqueness. We will be proactive in our responsiveness to any factor that may affect—not that *will* affect—students' development and learning. We leave nothing to chance.

Competency 003 supports the same concept in relation to integrity, fairness, and ethics because the principal promotes awareness of learning differences, multicultural awareness, gender sensitivity, and ethnic appreciation. All of these are diversity factors. The point is basic: The development and learning of every student is paramount. We are here for each of them, regardless of who they are or whether they have 16 tattoos or green hair. Ensuring responsiveness to diversity that may affect students' development and learning shall be addressed because the principal is ensuring that it will be.

This is indeed an ethics issue. Educators who do not have strong convictions about responding to anything that affects students' development and learning should look for a new career.

Guess My Favorites

I have two particular favorites in this competency.

- Facilitate the implementation of sound, research-based instructional strategies, decision, and programs in which multiple opportunities to learn and be successful are available to all students.
- Ensure responsiveness to diverse sociological, linguistic, cultural, and other factors that may affect students' development and learning.

Important Points to Remember

- The principal is the shepherd of the school, advocating, nurturing, and sustaining everything that affects student learning and staff professional growth.
- All students, regardless of any factor, must have multiple research-based opportunities to learn and be successful.
- It is important to create conditions that nurture and sustain a supportive campus climate and culture focused on student learning and staff professional development.
- Formative and summative assessment data must be used from many different sources to facilitate informed decision making.
- Campus goals must be aligned with the budget and vice versa. The same is true for curriculum with assessment and campus needs with staff development.
- Technology should be integrated everywhere.
- Student activities and programs directly affect academic, developmental, social, and cultural needs and are an important part of the campus culture and climate.
- Respond appropriately to anything with the potential to affect students in any way.
- Sustain the stewardship of student and staff success.

Human Resources Leadership and Management

Domain II: Instructional Leadership

Domain Key Concepts: Curriculum, Instruction, Staff Development

Competency 006

The principal knows how to implement a staff evaluation and development system to improve the performance of all staff members, select and implement appropriate models for supervision and staff development, and apply the legal requirements for personnel management.

Principals are evaluators of all staff on their campuses. Although others may also evaluate some employees such as maintenance and custodial workers, the principal is still primarily responsible for staff evaluation. Most, but not all, Texas school districts participate in the Professional Development Assessment System for the evaluation of teachers. Districts may use an alternative assessment system provided it meets state guidelines. Regardless, teachers are evaluated through a consistent district assessment system. Administrators must be trained and certified in the district model before they can assess teachers. Likewise, all other staff members fall into various district-selected evaluation processes. The responsibility therefore lies with the principal to implement a staff evaluation and development system. The purpose of staff evaluation and development systems is to improve the performance of all staff members.

Although all principals participate in staff evaluation, they do not always follow through with the second piece of this directive: development. Although everyone is willing to give lip service to staff development, in the busyness of leading and managing a school, staff development is often neglected. How can we nurture and sustain growth for students if we do not make a conscientious effort to plan for the nurturance and growth of staff? This may not make sense, but it happens. It's usually not intentional but more a case of the "squeaky wheel getting the oil." Other things appear to be more pressing, more immediate, and more tangible.

Regardless, this is wrong. We must feed the flock. How can we expect teachers to nurture and sustain students if we do not nurture and sustain teachers? This is done through a systematic plan for staff development. It doesn't consist of putting listings of regional service center course offerings in their boxes and hoping they will attend. Professional development activities for all staff members must be planned and included in the campus budget. Individual and campus needs assessments, personal assessments, disaggregation of testing and other campus data, community input, and other factors must be analyzed, discussed, planned, budgeted, implemented, and evaluated. As always, each component of individual and total staff development should be followed by the question, "How can we do it better?" This key question is a starting point for reflection, analysis, and action research on any topic.

When we finish something, say, an annual project, it's easy to consider our responsibility over for the time being. This is wrong—we're only half way there. Unless we ask ourselves how we can do it better next time, we'll keep doing what we've always done. And if we keep doing what we've always done, we'll keep getting what we've always gotten. We can—and must—do better. Staff development at the personal and campus level is the starting point for curricular, instructional, campus, and personal growth. It's a necessity to stop a potentially great school from becoming just another status quo campus. We want positive, proactive campuses ready to lead the charge for a better society. If we are not proactively planning for individual and campus development, our actions say we are content with what we have. Are you? If not, implement a staff evaluation and development system to improve the performance of all staff members.

As a part of this process, principals must select and implement appropriate models for supervision and staff development. Regardless of the evaluation system in place for teachers and other staff members, principals must make sure they are using an appropriate model. This will be determined by individual campus needs as well as by district policy. Nonetheless, two things are always required: visibility and communication. Principals cannot isolate themselves in their offices. They must proactively make the time to be visible in classrooms, halls, gymnasiums, the cafeteria, and everywhere else. The "MBWA model" (management by wandering around) has great merit. Staff and students need to see you on a regular basis, outside your office, actively involved on campus and in the community. They must see you "walk the walk" of professional development by seeking to develop yourself. Not only should you seek to learn, you should actively communicate and share what you've learned. Communication is a strong key in keeping every channel of opportunity and dialogue open. Open, consistent communication can avert or ease most problems, and routine visibility facilitates this communication.

Development opportunities are not limited to attending conferences or workshops. Reading good books and literature, keeping abreast of current research and best practices, inviting guest speakers to the school, or visiting other campuses to see how they address similar issues are examples of professional development. Always follow up development activities with frank, open discussion. Remember, communication is everything. We learn from each other. We grow together. We share insights. Sometimes we agree, and sometimes we don't. The campus benefits from collective discussion and collaboration on current issues and trends, but without a systematic, planned effort toward growth and development, we don't have enough information for discussion.

Principals must be prepared to face the less positive aspects of management as well. Staff observations, walk-throughs, and documentation are essential to leadership, but they also must be legal. Principals must know and apply the legal requirements for personnel management. You may want to fire an employee on the spot, but unless he or she has done something outside significant policy or legal guidelines, you simply cannot. You must document and provide due process. You must follow established campus and district policy. You must follow the chain of command. Make it your business to know district policy and legal parameters. You do not want to guess at a critical moment.

Furthermore, as a part of staff development, be sure your entire faculty and staff members are cognizant of any legal or policy changes that take place. Ignorance of the law is not an acceptable excuse. It can also get you into a lot of trouble. It's difficult to improve the world one school at a time when you've been fired for making a stupid mistake. Make sure you apply the legal requirements for personnel management and every other aspect of school leadership.

The Principal Knows How To . . .

- *Work collaboratively with other campus personnel to develop, implement, evaluate, and revise a comprehensive campus professional development plan that addresses staff needs and aligns professional development with identified goals.*

Part of the vision of the school must include the professional development of all staff members. If we as professionals are not growing and developing, we are standing still. If we are standing still, we become stagnant. Therefore, it is imperative that the development of all staff members, including yourself, be considered, planned for, implemented, evaluated, and funded.

The first step is a needs assessment to determine the actual versus perceived needs and interests of the staff. Once these are identified, collaborate with other campus personnel to develop, implement, evaluate, and revise a comprehensive campus professional development plan.

This four-step model—develop, implement, evaluate, revise—is evident in various forms throughout the competencies. First, we develop the plan. Next, we implement it. It accomplishes nothing to have a plan on paper or to present it to the school board but never to put it into action. Next, we evaluate it. Nothing is perfect—anything worth doing is worth evaluating. It is through evaluation, assessment, and measurement that we determine the value of the program, plan, model, curriculum, or teaching strategy we're implementing. Once we know a project's strengths and weaknesses, we finish the process by completing the necessary revisions to make it more efficient, timely, and productive. Staff development, as with everything else that occurs in our schools, must be directly linked to campus-identified goals. The evaluation process is one tool to ensure we are making measurable progress toward their attainment. Figure 8.1 illustrates the flow of campus needs, viewed as the foundation on which staff development is built. Staff development should directly connect to campus goals and vision attainment.

Campus Needs ⟶ Staff Development ⟶ Goals ⟶ Vision

Figure 8.1. Campus Success Flowchart

- *Facilitate the application of adult learning principles and motivation theory to allow campus professional development activities, including the use of appropriate content, processes, and contexts.*

Faculty and other staff members are adult learners and must be treated as such. They have their own unique set of motivations and inhibitors. Principals and central office administrators who work on staff development activities must base them on adult learning principles and motivation theory. In addition, keep in mind that adults appreciate having food and drinks at after-school meetings. They are tired and usually ready to go home. Attending after-school meetings is usually not at the top of their "Fun Things to Do in the Afternoon" list. Snacks show appreciation and give them energy to keep going through the afternoon meeting. Busy adults also appreciate well-planned meetings that do not require them to stay for hours at a time. In-depth discussions, brainstorming, and problem solving should be scheduled for other times. All staff development programs should include the use of appropriate content, processes, and contexts. It should be relevant and meaningful. It should have purpose. It should be on their level. Most of all, it should be interesting and relate to personal and campus goals. Anything less is a waste of valuable time that none of us has to spare.

- *Allocate appropriate time, funding, and other needed resources to ensure the effective implementation of professional development plans.*

Time is a common denominator for virtually everything that takes place in school. It is also one of the first things to be neglected in planning. Without time to study, discuss, and plan, it doesn't matter if a school is the richest in the state or if teachers have every conceivable curriculum and resource at their fingertips. Teachers must have time to pilot and evaluate the curriculum in their classrooms. Time supercedes everything. Watch for TExES answers that capitalize on this concept. Time management is critical. Good principals know and help teachers "get out of the box" by planning creative ways to use their time. Principals must then allocate appropriate time, funding, and other needed resources to ensure (remember *ensure?*) the effective implementation of professional development plans.

Although funding, budgeting, and resource management are addressed specifically in Domain III, it is important to connect them to staff development in Domain II. Similar to time procurement and management, we won't get very far without appropriate funding and other needed resources (see Figure 3.1).There have been quite a few lawsuits addressing school finance equity to prove that point. Although progress on the state level has been made, the issue is far from settled. In the meantime, principals must ensure that all resources are aligned with the campus vision and goals. This includes time for planning, study, observations, conferencing, and so forth. Every resource included in the budget must be aligned with at least one campus goal. The reverse is also true. All resources necessary to implement strategies, programs, and so forth toward campus goal attainment must be identified and included in the budget (see Figures 3.1–3.6). Without both pieces of this equation, appropriate resources will not be forthcoming and available. In the end, students will not have appropriate resources for learning, and staff members will not have the appropriate resources for growth and development. The budget must be aligned with campus goals, and resources must be used and managed appropriately.

- *Implement effective, appropriate, and legal strategies for the recruitment, screening, selection, assignment, induction, development, evaluation, promotion, discipline, and dismissal of campus staff.*

We have already discussed the importance of making sure that everything you do is legal. There are federal and state laws that provide the operational framework. There are also local district policies that must be implemented effectively and appropriately. Law and policy go hand in hand to provide the basic operational structure of schools (Figure 8.2).

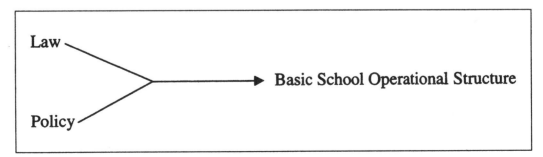

Figure 8.2. Law and Policy Provide a School's Basic Operational Structure

To have the best faculty and staff possible, principals must go beyond the basics. Teachers and other staff members must be recruited, screened, selected, and assigned to positions for which their strengths have best been identified. There is a shortage of certified teachers. We must have a system in place to find the best available and make them want to be part of our team. After all, ours are positive, future-oriented campuses where the focus is on doing what is best for all students. Why should the best and the brightest want to work anywhere else?

Once the best teachers are hired, we cannot just welcome them to the campus, give them the keys, and wish them well. Education is seriously lacking in the area of induction. Induction is more than orientation. It means helping new employees acclimate to the life, culture, campus, and values of the school. It means helping them with the ups and downs of being a new and integral part of the campus. It demands supportive mentoring rather than just well-wishing. It demands taking time and a personal interest in helping them succeed. When teachers succeed, so do students. We have a vested interest in helping all teachers grow and do their best. Part of doing their best is helping them become engaged members of a learning community. In so doing, everyone wins. It becomes a "win-win" situation. I'm all for "win-win" situations—and so are the test developers, so watch for answers that use them on the test.

- *Use formative and summative evaluation procedures to enhance the knowledge and skills of campus staff.*

It is morally and ethically wrong to wait until an end-of-the-year summative evaluation to play "gotcha!" with a teacher's assessment. It also isn't fair to the students who are supposed to have been learning from that teacher all along. How can any principal justify that? There should never be any surprises at summative conferences or at contract time if everyone is doing what they should be doing.

So what should they be doing? The best principals are in and out of classrooms all the time. They are there for more than formal evaluations. They are in and out doing walk-throughs. They are in and out saying hello. They are in and out for the sheer pleasure of watching teachers teach and watching students learn. They love every minute of it, just as people who appreciate fine music enjoy really good concerts. To these principals, being in classrooms is not a burden, it's sheer pleasure. It's why they come to school every day. They do not come to take care of budgets and discipline. They do not come to make sure the buses are running on time. They are not there to calm down irate parents. They are there because they get to witness students finding their way in the world through magnificent teaching and learning.

For this to happen, these same principals work with teachers, aides, and other staff members on a continuous basis, always looking for ways to enhance curriculum, instruction, programs, facilities, and the learning environment. These are not things that occur easily or overnight. They are nurtured and developed over time. There are no quick fixes. Everything truly valuable develops over time. Think of it like going on a diet. If someone is overweight by 100 pounds and they start a diet, they do not expect to lose it all by next week. They didn't gain the weight overnight, nor will they lose it overnight. What they must do is develop a weight reduction plan, then stick with it. Slowly and with great effort, they begin to lose weight.

The same is true in our schools. Teachers did not develop poor instructional strategies or a bad attitude overnight. Well, sometimes we think they developed a bad classroom climate overnight. But usually it took time. It will take them time to change. We cannot expect an entire campus to change overnight. We can expect the campus to make slow and steady gains in the right direction, through formative and summative evaluation and feedback, such that incremental gains will begin to occur, pick up momentum, and eventually become the new culture of the school. Success breeds success. Praise the tiniest of baby steps forward. Encourage innovation. Celebrate whatever you can find to celebrate until the bigger things start to occur. By using formative and summative evaluation procedures to enhance the knowledge and skills of the campus staff, teaching, learning, climate, and productivity will be enhanced.

- *Diagnose campus organizational health and morale and implement strategies to provide ongoing support to campus staff.*

As we discussed in Domain I, good culture and climate alone may not make you, but they sure can break you. They are essential to campus organizational health and morale. This is why implementing strategies to provide ongoing support to campus staff is so important. There are various organizational health inventories available on the market today. Likewise, many schools, districts, and regional service centers have developed their own. Each realizes the value and importance of the health and morale of the school.

It isn't enough for a principal to know that the health and morale on his or her campus is pretty good or not so swell. Good principals are always in the process of dreaming up creative ways to implement strategies to provide ongoing support to campus staff. This is part of the stewardship of the vision from Domain I. We must feed the flock. We must nurture those who are in the trenches, day after day, getting the work done. We must provide support for those who are physically or emotionally drained from a particularly exhausting day, week, month, or even a really tough year. It happens. It doesn't mean that you turned into a crummy principal or that your entire staff lost complete reason all at the same time. Sometimes the problem is circumstance. Other times it just seems like plain old bad luck. Some people might argue that there is no such thing as bad luck, that we create our own circumstances. Regardless, it's up to the principal to hold sacred the stewardship of the campus vision and to always look for ways to provide ongoing support by touching the hearts, lives, and minds of all campus staff. In the ideal school everyone is at his or her best every day. In reality, that probably isn't the case, but it is our goal. It's what we strive for. Our best chance of getting there is to safeguard our organizational health and morale.

- *Engage in ongoing professional development activities to enhance one's own knowledge and skills and to model lifelong learning.*

We have discussed the professional development of all staff members at great length. But what about yours? Who is supposed to nurture and support the principal?

Well, folks, that's a very good question. Some would argue that no one nurtures and supports the principal, that it is a thankless job, and that there is significant truth to the old adage that it's lonely at the top. Too often, this is true. But that will not stop you. You are never to be daunted. You know that others will value what they see you value. You know that your walk must match your talk. Therefore, you desire and look forward to engaging in ongoing professional development activities to enhance your own knowledge and skills and to model lifelong learning.

That sounds like a mouthful, but in truth it is one of the best parts of all the competencies. You want to be actively learning, sharing what you have learned, encouraging others to step out of their own comfort zones, and try new things. They will be more willing to give it a try themselves because they see you doing it. They see you actively, regularly, and enthusiastically sharing what you have learned, what you wish you knew, and how you plan to learn more about whatever interests or will benefit your campus. You are the living, breathing role model of personal professional development. People imitate what they see being practiced successfully. It's been said that imitation is the most sincere form of flattery. This is one place where ego is not the issue. You want them to copy you like crazy! You want them to read, discuss, practice, attend meetings and conferences, reflect, and try new things all the time. What better motivator could they have than a growing, continuously learning principal who is excited to communicate and articulate everything they are learning?

Now, let's discuss professional development from a strictly selfish point of view. In addition to wanting to learn and grow for the benefit of your campus and staff, you want to learn and grow just because you are in love with learning. You will likely be reading a book or listening to a tape the day you die. You are pumped up for learning, and it shows in every facet of your personal and professional life. Your mind is sharp and quick. You are well versed in myriad issues. You can articulate intelligently as a proponent of education for all and on the continued development of a free and democratic society. In other words, you have your act together and are one class act, pardon the pun. Furthermore, you expect the same from students, faculty, and everyone else.

You can participate in growth activities in countless ways. The only limitation is your creativity. Obvious choices are membership and participation in professional organizations on the local, state, and national level. All the educational organizations publish wonderful journals, newsletters, and other media. You receive these simply by being a member. Make it a practice to read something from these every week. You will be surprised how your knowledge of critical issues and the ways they affect your school will improve. Then you can share that knowledge with your campus and facilitate discussion on its relevancy to your school. You can then collaboratively address how to apply it. Conversation and discourse produce a diversity of thought and reflection. Both are good things. Anything that gets people thinking and talking is a good thing—communication builds camaraderie and teamwork; it facilitates the nurturance of the learning community.

The professional organizations also sponsor local, state, and national conferences every year. Students frequently ask me what organization is better, the National Association of Secondary School Principals (NASSP) and its state affiliate, the Texas Association of Secondary School Principals (TASSP), or their elementary counterparts, the National Association of Elementary School Principals (NAESP) and the Texas Elementary Principals and Supervisors Association (TEPSA). They are all excellent, and I'm a member of all of them. If I were still a principal, I would join the one for the area in which I was currently working. Middle school people, you're in luck. All these organizations want you!

In addition to the specific principals' organizations, there are many other worthwhile associations. Two of these are the Association for Supervision and Curriculum Development (ASCD) and Phi Delta Kappa (PDK). Although not specific to principals, both focus on the improvement and timely dissemination of information regarding education. There are others, of course, such as the American Association of School Administrators (AASA) and the Texas Association of School Administrators (TASA), the primary focus of which is the superintendency. Nonetheless, many principals and central office people are members of these organizations and benefit greatly from their publications and conferences. The most important thing is not which organizations you join or support, but that you are taking advantage of the opportunities for learning that they provide. You will be surprised at how much your knowledge and expertise increase simply by reading the things they send you in the mail, without ever having to step into a conference. But I strongly encourage you to attend as many conferences as you can. You will benefit physically, cognitively, and emotionally. They will lift you up and recharge you. Can you think of a better reason to attend?

As I said, professional development activities are only limited by your creativity. They can be as simple as visiting a local or nearby school with similar circumstances or demographics or a school that is using a program or teaching strategy in which your campus is interested. Take teachers and other staff members with you. These visits are usually close to home and therefore inexpensive, but they are invaluable. Always remember to share what you have learned. It multiplies the benefits. Plus, it lets your campus know that you did not simply take the day off to have a nice long lunch without them—not that an ideal principal would even think of such a thing. Let teachers see your credibility.

Do all of this until the day you die. Direct your family to have inscribed on your tombstone, "He [or she] lived to learn." Never stop growing and learning. It will keep you sharp. It will keep you from losing focus of what is going on in our field. It will keep you from becoming stagnant.

Guess My Favorite

It surely will not take a Rhodes scholar to figure out this one. My favorite is this:

- Engage in ongoing professional development activities to enhance one's own knowledge and skills and to model lifelong learning.

If this weren't my favorite, my walk wouldn't match my talk, would it?

Important Points to Remember

- Focus all staff evaluation and development activities on helping everyone achieve his or her potential.
- Staff evaluation and development should be from a helpful versus a "gotcha" perspective.
- Time is the common denominator. Without it, other resources cannot be maximized.
- Mentoring and other induction activities are critical to the acclimation of new staff members to the campus culture and values. Help them find their place as an important part of the learning community.
- Make your staff feel appreciated and valued.
- Facilitate ways to retain good people.
- Facilitate growth for all members of the campus community.
- Assessment should occur in every avenue of the school, including personnel. People address what is measured. Help people succeed.
- The stewardship of the vision is your responsibility. Others can and should help, but it is your responsibility.
- Read, study, learn, attend professional conferences, and grow until the day you die.

Learner-Centered Organizational Leadership and Management

Domain II: Instructional Leadership

Domain Key Concepts: Curriculum, Instruction, Staff Development

Competency 007

The principal knows how to apply organizational, decision-making, and problem-solving skills to ensure an effective learning environment.

An effective learning environment is the key to success on every campus. Research in virtually every area of organizational leadership points to the importance of culture and climate to productivity. This concept is stressed in Domain I as well as reiterated in Competency 005. It should come as no surprise that it is also important to organizational, decision-making, and problem-solving skills.

Throughout the domains and competencies, collaboration has been stressed. Collaboration sounds nice, but can it always exist without conflict? No, it cannot. If you have conflict within your school, is that always a bad thing? No, it is not. Without conflict, there is no diversity of thought. Without diversity of thought, how can we be challenged to confront long-held beliefs that may or may not apply or even be true? How can we grow? How can we address school improvement through change if we have no discourse to prod us to examine our attitudes, viewpoints, and practices? How can we make things better?

Principals should facilitate discussion and collaboration, not dictate it. Principals must lead by example. Remember, good leaders make others want to follow. Respect is not commanded. It is earned. For this to occur, principals must know about, possess, and be able to apply organizational, decision-making, and problem-solving skills. We cannot go into the ideal school and expect things to be rosy all the time. They can't be when schools filled with imperfect human beings. Interpersonal conflicts will occur. The reason some schools get closer to the ideal than others is that their leaders are trained to resolve conflict, to encourage dialogue and innovation, and always to seek better ways of doing things. If we keep on doing what we've always done, we'll keep on getting what we always have.

That's not good enough. To improve, we must read, study, think, reflect, and talk. Collaboratively, we also have to make difficult choices and decisions, deciding which path to take, which curriculum to chose, which instructional strategies are best for individual children, which model of professional development is best for a specific employee, and so forth. These decisions do not always come easily. Often, there are no perfect answers. We must make choices. Sometimes we end up regretting decisions and wishing we could change them. In those cases, it isn't a crime to say, "We messed up," and then go back and readdress the issue. The real crime would be to keep doing something that either isn't working or is just plain wrong simply because "That's my story, and I'm sticking to it." What a pitiful way to run a school. The ideal principal is always formatively and summatively assessing everything to find ways to improve. The ideal principal is never afraid to regroup and do things differently by applying organizational, decision-making, and problem-solving skills to ensure an effective learning environment. There is no other way.

The Principal Knows How To . . .

- *Implement appropriate management techniques and group process skills to define roles, assign functions, delegate authority, and determine accountability for campus goal attainment.*

The ideal principal knows there's a fine balance between using a collaborative, open-door leadership style and empowering others in organizational, decision-making, and problem-solving skills. The principal accomplishes this balance by putting specific strategies in place to help others understand their roles within the school community. The ideal principal not only defines roles, functions, and responsibilities but also makes sure team members buy into, understand, and accept them. Authority and acceptance for decision making must be clearly understood such that teachers or others will not "pass the buck," thereby undermining accountability for campus goal attainment.

Remember the old saying, "Be careful what you ask for? You just might get it"? Sometimes that happens when there's a change in leadership style and philosophy. Sometimes teachers, staff members, and the community may think they want a collaborative style, yet without appropriate planning, development, training, and implementation, it can become a great big bust. They simply weren't ready for it. People need to be sure they want new responsibilities, then they need to be trained before they can be held accountable for the results. Too often, there are two types of breakdowns that occur:

1. Stakeholders thought they wanted empowerment but realized that with empowerment comes a lot of hard work for which they were unprepared.
2. Stakeholders really do want to be a part of the decision-making process but are not equipped with the skills to be successful.

Therefore, for the organization to be productive and effective, the principal must facilitate in-depth discussion of the campus vision and of the goals and training to attain that vision. The principal then must provide practice and techniques to ensure those goals are reached.

- *Implement procedures for gathering, analyzing, and using data from a variety of sources for informed campus decision making.*

Well, look here. It's our old pal triangulation again. We are once more trying to look at data from a variety of sources to make prudent, informed decisions based on fact rather than perception, prejudice, or bias. Great principals do not make "seat-of-the-pants" decisions. They do not ask a single person's opinion or look at a single test score or a single anything else. They look at many different sources to make informed decisions. They do this by implementing procedures for gathering, analyzing, and using data from a variety of sources for informed campus decision making.

- *Frame, analyze, and resolve problems using appropriate problem-solving techniques and decision-making skills.*

Here is another example of integration and overlapping of roles within the principalship. Principals must use various sources of data to make appropriate decisions. They must also use this data to frame, analyze, and resolve problems. To frame a problem means to spell it out, to clearly define it, and to study its different facets to see where the conflicts are. Writing things out is one way to do this. There is something about having to structure thoughts and issues into specific sentences and paragraphs that makes them clearer. Psychologists and counselors recommend journal writing as a form of proactive therapy and conflict resolution for this reason. It brings things to light, letting you identify problems and brainstorm their solutions in a safe manner. Writing things out helps those involved to analyze the problem and its potential solutions. In analyzing a situation, there are no bad ideas. Everyone's input is welcomed, respected, and considered. All of this comes together to find a healthy way to resolve the problem. If this solution doesn't work, we try another. The important thing is to never give up. We just keep on trying and trying and trying until we get it right. We try not to become discouraged when we fall down. We always remember to get back up. We just keep right on framing, analyzing, and resolving until we come up with the right resolution to solve or improve the problem.

- *Use strategies for promoting collaborative decision making and problem solving, facilitating team building, and developing consensus.*

It all boils down to collaboration. Collaboration is an important sign of a healthy campus culture and climate, as stressed repeatedly in Domain I. We have to talk to each other. No problems were ever solved and no consensus was ever reached by shutting others out and thinking, "The other people at this school are complete idiots. They don't know squat. I must be the only reasonable person here because those others are crazy!"

You and I both know this attitude exists. It may not be that pronounced, but it tends to multiply if given an opportunity. To prevent this, serious planning and resources must be put into the creation of strategies that promote collaborative decision making and problem solving, that facilitate team building, and that develop consensus. Think about Domain I for this one, because it's all about the culture and climate of the school. Planning and resources must be put into developing conflict resolution skills, facilitating the concept of the school as a team, and tools to develop consensus. We may not always agree on everything that happens or even how we will deal with it, but we do agree that this is the plan we're going to try first. All team members will support the plan even if it was not their choice. If it doesn't work, we'll try something else. But for the moment, this is what we have agreed to support. That means we give this idea 100% of our effort. We do not sit back, making only a minimal effort and watching the plan fail, then smugly say, "I told them that wouldn't work." We turn that negativity into collaboration. We come up with a plan that may not be perfect but that everyone can support and to which everyone will give optimal effort. In so doing, our schools will reap the benefits of collaborative decision making and problem solving, team building, and consensus.

- *Encourage and facilitate positive change, enlist support for change, and overcome obstacles to change.*

We have discussed the concept of the principal as nurturer and cheerleader of the school as well as champion of the stewardship of the vision. How is this done? It's done by knowing that regardless of what happens every single day, you will encourage everyone in a positive manner. You will go beyond encouraging to facilitating, ensuring that change occurs. You will enlist support for change from every element of the school community. You will be on your feet, busy, and proactive. You will not be sitting in your office sipping tea or wondering if the Cowboys will ever get their act together again. In fact, you may have a few things you'd like to share with the Cowboys about team building. Forget the Cowboys and forget sipping tea. There will be days when you do not even have time for lunch and only dream about getting home for supper. You are too busy out in the trenches, encouraging and facilitating positive change, enlisting support for change, and overcoming obstacles to change. There always have been obstacles to change, and there always will be.

If we let the obstacles stand in our way, we are accepting the status quo and thereby saying that change cannot occur, that we cannot create a better school, and that we cannot touch lives.

Is that what you really want? Is that what our children deserve? Is that the attitude we need to change the world, one great school at a time? Absolutely not. It's up to us to get out there, get dirty, get physically and emotionally involved, and overcome obstacles. We will not let obstacles be excuses. We want to make Popsicles out of obstacles. We want them to melt on the sidewalks under our feet as we hurry along, making a difference. We will never give up. We will never be defeated. We are positive change agents out changing the world. Those obsolete status quo principals can sit on a tack and bemoan the fate of society. We cannot. We will be the ones to make the difference. We will do this very simply. Every single day we will get out there with everyone we meet to encourage and facilitate positive change, enlist support for change, and overcome obstacles to change. We will develop a thick skin when people tell us we're wasting our time. We will ask them if they have a better way than ours. Somehow I bet that they do not. They are either intimidated or scared to death by our passion. They know that to be a part of our team will mean work. They will not be able to slough off responsibility at children's expense. At our school, change is in the air, and we are here to make it happen.

- *Apply skills for monitoring and evaluating change and making needed adjustments to achieve goals.*

So while we are on our ongoing quest for excellence, how will we know we are making any progress and not just exhausting ourselves while treading water? We will have a system in place to constantly monitor and evaluate change. What does this mean? It means we will be formatively and summatively engaged in action research. It means we will always ask ourselves and others how we can measure progress or the lack of it. We will establish criteria to measure change and to determine whether that change has been positive or negative.

To do this, we must have a plan. Remember, we do not come up with this plan by ourselves. We must empower our learning team to identify criteria and benchmarks while developing a process to evaluate everything we do on our campuses. If what we are doing works, terrific. But we aren't done. How can we make it even better?

If what we are doing is not working, what really serious things can we do to help it succeed? What can we modify to make it better? After identifying specific strategies, costs must be determined. Are our plans cost-effective? Can we afford them? If not, are there things we can modify to facilitate these methods, ideas, or programs instead of something else? If we cannot afford our new ideas this year, what strategies should we undertake to guarantee that the needed resources are provided for in next year's budget? The most important thing is to always ask ourselves how we can improve everything we do on a daily basis. Is this exhausting? Yes. Will it wear you down? Of course. You are human. But is it necessary to the ultimate productivity of your school as evidenced in the teaching and learning of teachers and students? You bet it is.

Guess My Favorite

Well, this certainly should come as no surprise. My favorite is the following:

- Encourage and facilitate positive change, enlist support for change, and overcome obstacles to change.

If we are not encouragers and facilitators of positive change in our schools, we are in the wrong business. Our schools must have people who are committed to being proactive change agents, enlisting others along the way, and who never let a dumb old obstacle or bureaucrat get in their way. Keep your eyes on the vision. Never give up.

Important Points to Remember

- Collaborate!
- Use as many people and as many data sources as possible to empower and make informed decisions. Show me the data!
- Make a system to evaluate, modify, and improve everything. Nothing is exempt. There are no sacred cows. Everything is subject to improvement.
- What is measured gets done. Having a personal program and a goal-attainment accountability system are essential to growth.
- The team's the thing. Schools are joint ventures of multiple people forming a team, a family, with common goals toward the attainment of the campus vision.
- Never, ever, ever, in a billion years give up.

The Business and Technology of School Leadership and Management

Domain III: Administrative Leadership

Domain Key Concepts: Finance, Facilities, Safety

Competency 008

The principal knows how to apply principles of effective leadership and management in relation to campus budgeting, personnel, resource utilization, financial management, and technology use.

We have now entered Domain III, Administrative Leadership. This is our final domain. It includes Competencies 008 and 009. Both are shorter and more managerial in nature. In fact, the only places you'll find the word *management* in a competency definition is in Competencies 008 and 009. There is a difference between leadership and management. Leadership looks to the future and is visionary. Management is directed at the daily operation of the organization. Some people are visionary leaders but do not have the skills to manage the details and mechanics of running the school.

Others are the opposite. They are excellent at paper-and-pencil tasks and organization, but they have no vision. Separately, neither is good enough for the ideal school. Today's principal must be a leader and a manager. The ideal principal must be the steward of the school's vision but also able to manage the details of attaining it. This is a classic example of leadership being both a skill and an art. The work of leading and managing, as portrayed in Domain III, is both an art and a skill. The descriptions are short, to the point, and more businesslike in nature than the competencies in Domains I and II. The key common themes are finance, facilities, and safety.

In Competency 008, the principal knows how to apply principles of effective leadership and management in relation to campus budgeting, personnel, resource use, financial management, and technology use. It is clear and straightforward. To manage the school, the principal must be a steward of the campus budget, knowing how to collaboratively set goals and allocate resources appropriately so that teachers and other staff members have what they need to reach those goals. The principal must plan for appropriate personnel recruitment, retention, and development. The principal must see to it that available resources are used prudently and that the entire campus budget is solvent. Although technology has been previously mentioned in the examples of principal performance, this is the first time it has been directly addressed in the definition of a competency. Technology is of growing importance in both teaching and learning. It is used in various ways, often involving legal regulations. It is the responsibility of the principal to see that it is used efficiently, effectively, safely, and legally.

The Principal Knows How To . . .

- *Apply procedures for effective budget planning and management.*

The budget should be planned with collaborative input and be aligned with campus goals (see Figure 3.1). Management of the budget requires consistent prudence in terms of funds and expenditures, as well as legal and policy regulations regarding all curricular and cocurricular accounts.

- *Work collaboratively with stakeholders to develop campus budgets.*

The campus budget should be developed collaboratively with various stakeholders in the school community. It should not be a well-guarded secret kept in the office under strict confidentiality. Goals and priorities for expenditures should be planned and developed together. Stakeholders should be empowered in the development and use of the budget. Nonetheless, the principal is ultimately responsible for the fiscal integrity of expenditures and accountability.

- *Acquire, allocate, and manage human, material, and financial resources according to district policies and campus priorities.*

There is more to campus budgeting than money. It is the responsibility of the principal to acquire, allocate, and manage human and material resources as well as financial resources. This includes personnel and curricular resources. All resources must be acquired, allocated, and managed according to district policies and campus priorities as collaboratively developed in the campus vision and district policies.

- *Apply laws and policies to ensure sound financial management in relation to accounts, bidding, purchasing, and grants.*

The principal must apply principles of effective leadership and management in applying laws and policies to ensure sound financial management in all areas. Different districts use different accounting programs and procedures. Each district has its own policies within state and federal regulations. It is the responsibility of the principal to ensure that all laws and policies are consistently and prudently enforced.

- *Use effective planning, time management, and organization of personnel to maximize attainment of district and campus goals.*

Having all the material resources in the world will not maximize student learning without effective time management and organization. Planning for time management is often overlooked, yet without time to plan, study, develop, conference, and collaborate, no person or campus can maximize attainment of anything. Empower your school community to develop innovative ways to maximize time management. It is an essential component in the attainment of your campus vision.

- *Develop and implement plans for using technology and information systems to enhance school management.*

Where would we be without technology in all its various forms today? The principal must facilitate the development and implementation of plans for using technology and information systems to enhance school management. The Public Education Information Management System, more commonly called PEIMS, data are just one type of information system. Clerical staff members are usually responsible for entering these data, but many people are responsible for supplying and checking them. The principal must facilitate technology integration into curriculum and instruction—and throughout the school community. Legal issues, such as site licenses related to the use of designated software on more than one computer, must be consistently applied.

Guess My Favorite

Now this cannot possibly come as a surprise. My favorite is as follows:

- Work collaboratively with stakeholders to develop campus budgets.

Important Points to Remember

- Budget development begins with campus goal setting and prioritization.
- Budgets should be developed collaboratively.
- All legal regulations and district policies must be followed consistently.
- Never misappropriate funds!
- If teachers and other members of the school community do not have time to plan, study, and reflect, the campus will not achieve maximum productivity. Time management is critical.
- The use of technology and information systems is essential to school management.

The Physical Plant and Support Systems

Domain III: Administrative Leadership

Domain Key Concepts: Finance, Facilities, Safety

Competency 009

The principal knows how to apply principles of leadership and management to the campus physical plant and support systems to ensure a safe and effective learning environment.

There is no greater proof of how much society has changed than when a competency of principal effectiveness now has to address safety. In years gone by, school safety was assumed. Only under extremely remote circumstances did deliberate violence occur on school property. When the community thought of school safety, it was in relation to fire and weather drills. If the building and grounds met basic safety standards and appropriate drills were in place and documented, that was about as far as the issue of school safety was taken.

Unfortunately, this is no longer true. Many schools now have metal detectors. Districts have risk managers. Most secondary schools have some type of identification process for faculty and students, such as mandatory name tags. Many public school campuses are adopting more conservative dress codes or even uniforms in an attempt to reduce disciplinary problems and increase campus pride. Some schools even require see-through purses and backpacks so that weapons or other contraband can be seen. Virtually all schools have more restrictive policies for visitors. Many schools have security guards or police on campus at all times, particularly during extracurricular events. Yes, the world has changed. Not all of this change has been good.

We pray that a tragedy like that which occurred at Columbine High School will never happen again. Unfortunately, all the rules in the world cannot solve the underlying causes of school violence. I sincerely wish they could. I sincerely wish there were no need for these rules. I wish every child had a supportive home with parents who supplied them with all the necessities of life, including love, concern, and support. I wish socioeconomic differences, prejudice, bigotry, and other inequities did not exist. But they do.

We cannot prevent another Columbine. Hoping and wishing will not change the world. Rules will not change the world. All we can do is try—every day and in every way—to make *our* campuses safe and orderly places where teachers can teach and students can learn, where every adult exhibits a sincere interest in every young person, where each person feels valued. I told you that I believe in the ideal school. Having the ideal school is a matter of trying to do everything we can with our physical plant and support systems to ensure a safe and effective learning environment for all students and everyone else in the learning community.

The Principal Knows How To . . .

- *Implement strategies that enable the school physical plant, equipment, and support systems to operate safely, efficiently, and effectively.*

The principal must know how to apply principles of leadership and management to the campus by implementing strategies that enable the school physical plant, equipment, and support systems to operate safely, efficiently, and effectively. In simple language, everything at the school must be safe. All things must operate efficiently and effectively. This encompasses everything from vacuum cleaners to cafeteria, physical education, and life skills equipment. The floors and walls of the school must be clean and safe. There can be no mold or asbestos. The air within the buildings must also be clean and safe. Do not assume it's obvious that everything in the school should be safe, efficient, and effective for its designated task.

- *Apply strategies for ensuring the safety of students and personnel and for addressing emergencies and security concerns.*

Think Columbine, weather, fire, and other disasters, but don't forget other important student safety issues, such as who the custodial parent is, with whom a child can leave the school, and, perhaps more important, with whom a child *cannot* leave the school. Be cognizant of health issues, communicable diseases, and potential allergic reactions. Be sure you have a policy for every type of emergency—from illnesses to broken bones to tornadoes—and then make sure the school community uses that policy. It is your responsibility to ensure the safety of students and personnel and to address emergencies and security concerns. Most important, stay calm in the event of an emergency. You are in charge.

- *Develop and implement procedures for crisis planning and for responding to crises.*

This is another example of how you must have a plan—and then work the plan. It does no good to have a plan and then forget to use it during a panic situation. Stay calm. Everyone should have a defined, rehearsed role. In a crisis, everyone should immediately and effectively assume their role while being on full alert to help others. Student safety is our number one priority, but the safety of the entire faculty and staff is also paramount. You have a crisis management plan. Practice it, hope you never have to use it, but use it immediately and effectively should the need arise.

- *Apply local, state, and federal laws and policies to support sound decision making related to school programs and operations (e.g., student services, food services, health services, transportation).*

The first rule of thumb in the principalship is to stay legal. Always work within local, state, and federal laws and policies to support sound decision making related to school programs and operations. If you do not stay within these boundaries in every way, unfortunate things are likely to happen. Worse, you'll be unable to improve your school if you cause harm to a person or thing and are either placed on probation or fired. The ideal principal would never get fired.

Examples of school programs and operations include student services, food services, health services, and transportation, but this list is far from definitive. An easy way to remember what to include would be to delete the examples and insert the word *all* before school programs and operations. You want to make sound decisions in regards to all programs, operations, and problems. You want to be the wisest principal on the face of the Earth. You want to astound people with your wisdom. You want to live and breathe integrity, ethics, and fairness as described in Competency 003. The first step toward doing this is to always apply local, state, and federal laws and policies. If you are in doubt about the legality of an issue, never be afraid to ask for advice. It is better to ask and have the proper information to make an intelligent decision based on fact than to make a wrong decision based on presumption. It's better to be safe than sorry.

Guess My Favorite

This one is a complete no-brainer. It is basic to all school and organizational management.

- Apply local, state, and federal laws and policies to support sound decision making related to school programs and operations (e.g., student services, food services, health services, transportation).

Important Points to Remember

- Stay legal.
- Stay calm.
- Do not be afraid to ask for help.
- A wise decision based on facts is always better than a wrong decision based on presumption.
- Safety for all is paramount to the existence, culture, climate, and vision of the school.
- Have safety and crisis management plans developed, rehearsed, and ready in case of an emergency. Hope and pray you never have to use them.
- Have safety, efficiency, and effectiveness strategies consistently in place, practiced, and assessed for every facet of the school.

The Real Deal

Practical Application

Other Important Concepts
How Do I Read All That Data?

Data Analysis Simplified

Being able to analyze data is critical to your success as a principal and to passing the TExES. Yet, data analysis tends to scare people. It shouldn't. There are some basic tools to use that will help you get the "big picture" of what the data are saying. Remember, the TExES is built around knowledge and skills that an entry-level principal should have. You do not need to know how to disaggregate data for a doctoral dissertation to pass this test. Nonetheless, I firmly suggest that you do learn how to disaggregate data for the doctoral dissertation that I hope you'll complete one day. Doctorates are nice to have when you're attempting to change the world.

How to Read and Interpret Standardized Tests

There is no guarantee that you'll have a decision set built around standardized test results. But there's also no guarantee that you won't have a decision set built around standardized test results. Some people make a big mistake. They turn the page in their test booklet, see all those graphs, and think, "Here come those awful standardized tests." Their first response is to panic.

But not you. You are not going to panic. You know that when anxiety goes up, productivity goes down. You do not want your productivity to go down. After all, how can you be calm, cool, collected, confident, and downright cocky if you are panicking? Take a deep breath, blow it out slowly, and follow my suggestions.

Read the prompt for the decision set. It will lay the groundwork of what the decision set is all about. It will give you the feel of what the test developers are looking for. There is never anything to panic about in the prompt. All it does is to set you up. So read it and see what you're dealing with. Underline key words. Get the feel of the school you'll be analyzing.

Once you have done that, look at the charts or graphs provided. Think "big picture." At this point, you are interested only in the big picture. Standardized tests in these scenarios are usually achievement tests. They have been around longer than the Texas Assessment of Academic Skills (TAAS) and are something virtually every school in the nation deals with. You need to know how to interpret them.

Look at the chart or graph. For what grade or grade level are these data? Identify them. To what subject do the data refer? Identify this as well. Keep breathing slowly, deeply, and confidently. You are Rhett Butler from *Gone With the Wind*. Frankly, you don't care (although this isn't exactly what he said) what grade or subject it is except to be prepared for whatever questions may or may not be coming your way. Do not think, "Oh, my goodness! These are math scores! I hate math, and I doubly hate math scores!" Do not go there. It will not make one bit of difference if it's math, reading, or any other subject. Scores are scores. The real question is, what are you going to do with them?

Next, if there is a chart, look across the top and down the left side to see what your headings are. The headings will provide you with the categories of content that have been tested as well as the rating scales used.

Read the concepts on which the students have been tested. They likely will be grouped in broad categories. This will provide you the basic structure of what was tested. This helps constitute the big or global picture that you want to have before you start reading the questions within the decision set. Look next at the rating scales to see how they are categorized.

At this point, you will make some obvious conclusions ranging from, "This grade or school did pretty well" to "This grade or school did horribly. I need to be in charge of the school to turn it around!" You may notice some particular areas where the grade or school did very well or some areas where they did particularly poorly, which is a polite way of saying it stunk. More likely, the majority of the scores will be somewhere in between.

Stop here and listen to me. Do not try to be psychic with the decision set by thinking, "What else can I conclude from this data? What could they ask me? Oh, my goodness. I don't even know what these concepts stand for! What if they ask me something I do not know?" While you are doing that, two things are happening:

- While you are playing the "What If?" game, your anxiety level goes up. We all know by now what happens when your anxiety level goes up. Leave the "What If?" game alone. I will give you plenty of productive games to play in the next chapter. Right now, just identify the broad categories and move on. Do not try to read the minds of the test developers. After all, they were paid for developing the test. You were not.
- The clock is ticking. You have plenty of time to take and pass this test, but it makes no sense to waste it. There's no reason for you to sit there staring at all those data playing the "What If?" game. You do not want to wonder what comes next; you want to know. Turn the page to see for yourself what they're asking rather than fretting over "What If?" It is a better use of your limited time, it keeps you on track and focused, and it keeps you working with the clock instead of against it.

Remember, all you want to do is get the big picture of which data they are presenting, such as grade, subject, basic concepts tested, and a global view of how the school, grade, or class performed. Next, turn the page and get started on the questions. This test is a mind game. Do not let it psych you out. Beat it at its own game. Keep turning those pages.

The Big Surprise

Here is the big and pleasant surprise. In an entire decision set, rarely will they ask more than two or three questions that will actually have you go back and look at the data. The rest of the questions will be generic in nature, similar to questions in any other decision set. That is the surprise benefit of not getting yourself worked up over the data or playing the "What If?" game. Just go see what they really *are* asking you. This keeps your anxiety down and your productivity up; it makes the clock your friend instead of your enemy.

When you do come to the questions that actually have you go back and look at the data, you do not have to be a statistical whiz. They are looking for entry-level data analysis knowledge and skills. Therefore, if they ask you to pinpoint a large or the largest need in the school or grade, look for the lowest scores or scores on a downward trend. Low scores indicate the need for improvement (see Figure 12.1).

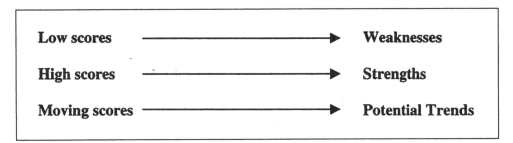

Figure 12.1. Interpreting Test Scores

Even the best schools have a lowest area in something. Until every school has 100% mastery of every concept on every test, there is always room to improve. This is a classic example of being a reflective and data-sensitive leader. Principals, teachers, and members of the school community must continuously ask themselves and others, "How can we do this better?" The "this" is generic. It makes no difference if we are discussing math scores, band competitions, or the Pillsbury Bake-Off. Until every student masters every objective, we are not there yet. We are not through seeking improvement. We do not have time to rest on our laurels, thinking like Scarlett O'Hara, "I'll think about it tomorrow at Tara." We must lead our schools today to prepare a democratic society for better tomorrows.

If a question steers you toward areas of growth within a school or grade, you should look at the numbers to see the greatest difference in a positive, not a negative, direction. If a question asks you where a school's greatest strengths are, look for the bigger numbers or the areas showing the greatest upward trends. It could be that one category of concepts or a certain grade is still higher than another, but that those scores are stagnant or even regressing a tiny bit. At the same time, another area may be showing consistent, steady—albeit slow—growth. If the numbers are consistently coming up, even slowly, it's a positive thing and should be noticed. Watch for answers that catch trends like that. The test developers love to throw in responses that determine if you are using higher-order thinking skills by catching trends or implications. Show them you are by selecting the correct response.

You will not be asked any detailed or advanced statistical analysis questions. This is not the primary role of the principal and certainly not of a beginning principal. The test will not ask you about variance or standard deviations. You will need to prove that you know how to determine whether students in your school are learning and what their strengths and weaknesses are. If students from all subgroups are not learning, why aren't they? What can be done to improve the culture, climate, instruction, and curriculum of the school such that all students can and do learn? The purpose of any student testing is threefold:

- To determine student growth
- To determine student and campus strengths, weaknesses, and trends
- To use this data as a sound basis for determining campus, grade, or subject goals for student growth and improvement

Last, remember that it doesn't matter how well your students score if *everyone* is not learning. Ideal principals never, never, never give up until every child is mastering every concept. School is not just for the motivated and easy to teach. It is for everyone. Do you think this philosophy is unrealistic? Fine. Maybe education isn't for you. There are plenty of jobs available for those who lack a passion for excellence in learning and for the propagation of a democratic society. You should be on a quest for educational excellence. If not, on the day of the test, pretend!

How to Read and Interpret an "Academic Excellence Indicator System" Report

Students all across the United States, in public and private schools, take achievement tests, but the Academic Excellence Indicator System (AEIS) is exclusive to Texas. Abbreviated district and campus reports may be easily accessed at www.tea.state.tx.us/preport/aeis/. An example report can be found at 222.judsonisd.org/parkvillage/general/AEIS.htm. You may find it helpful to visit these Web sites as you review this chapter to get a feel for the layout of the AEIS. Every school and district is rated with an accountability system based largely on data detailed in the AEIS report. Two important areas are student passing rates on the TAAS test and student attendance. Similar to standardized tests, there is no guarantee that you will or will not have decision sets based on AEIS results.[1] But by the time we get through discussing them, you'll be hoping for AEIS decision sets.

First, let's look at the big picture again. There are three specific areas to consider. You may or may not be given each of these components to analyze, but you want to know about all of them, just in case. First, there is the cover or title page. It will tell you the academic year of testing, as well as the name, campus number, and state rating of the school.

The actual report is divided into two sections. There are certain things that always appear in each section and that are never changed. Memorize them. If you know where to look for certain data, it will save you time and anxiety when responding to decision set questions.

The simplest way to remember the report is that everything about testing and attendance is in Section I. Everything else is in Section II (Figure 12.2). Therefore, when determining where to look for an appropriate answer, if the question does not relate to testing or student attendance, go straight to Section II and look in the appropriate category there. For ease in navigating the report, the section and page numbers are listed in the top right-hand corner of each page. Now, let's look deeper into what these things mean.

Section I of an AEIS Report

The first section of the AEIS report addresses everything you would ever want to know, or would not want to know, about student performance on TAAS in chart format. TAAS begins in the third grade and continues through the high school version. It is given primarily in reading, math, and writing,

SECTION I:	SECTION II:
Test Data	Student Information (except about testing)
Attendance	Staff Information
	Budget Information
	Program Information

Figure 12.2. Sections I and II of the Academic Excellence Indicator System

with secondary schools also reporting "End of Course Test" results. Although writing is taught in every grade, the writing test is not given at each grade level and thus will not be reported for certain grades. The "indicators" or student groups are listed at the top of the chart from left to right. It is helpful to think "big to little" in looking at the groupings. For the sake of our discussion, let's say we are looking at third-grade reading and math scores, since writing is not given in the third grade.

[1] Decision sets are the framework around which the TExES exam is built. A decision set consists of a short paragraph that describes a school situation. It is followed by various test questions that relate to that school situation.

The biggest group is the state. Under the column marked State, the scores of students per grade and subject, as appropriate for that report, will be listed. In our example of third grade, the column will show how all third graders in Texas did on reading and math. The next column will be labeled District. This column will show how the third graders in a specific district performed on reading and math.

The next column is Campus Group. The campus group is exceedingly important. It is second in importance only to the following column: your campus. What is the campus group? Each year, detailed demographic data about every student in every school as well as data about the school and district itself are entered by staff (not you, thank goodness) into the system called PEIMS (Public Education Information Management System). This system crunches all the numbers and codes for various factors such as students' race, gender, age, grade, socioeconomic status, and mobility, as well as district wealth and so forth. Each campus and district is given an opportunity to correct erroneous information at specific points during the year to ensure accuracy. It is in your campus's best interest for this information to be perfect because this is what is used to determine your campus group. The campus group includes the campuses in the state that are the most similar to yours according to all the factors indicated. You want to be in the correct campus group because your campus's performance will be compared with and contrasted to those in the AEIS report.

You may wonder why that is such a big deal. Let me explain. Let's say that you are principal of Poor Me Elementary. Poor Me is rather pitiful. One hundred percent of the students are on free or reduced lunch. No one speaks English. No one lives in a single-family dwelling. In fact, virtually everyone lives in low-rent property and often moves. Thus, students at your school are constantly changing. Few of the homes have two parents living in them. Unemployment and drugs abound. I am exaggerating, but you get the point. Poor Me Elementary has had dismal scores on all forms of student testing for years and has earned sympathy from the central administrative office, superintendent, and school board, because, gee, they are rather pitiful. Who could expect them to do well? They have been pitiful and gotten by without too much urging. It is a classic example of low expectations and reaping what you sow.

Well! The campus group has taken care of that. Poor Me Elementary is now being compared with other schools with demographics that look just like theirs. What principal would want to have to explain to their superintendent or other authority why their scores are worse than other schools that look just like them and have almost identical circumstances? The net result is, when the campus group variable went into effect, scores went up at Poor Me schools. Welcome to the world of accountability.

But, Poor Me schools are not the only ones affected. You did such a good job improving performance at Poor Me Elementary that you were transferred to Pretty Good Elementary. Pretty Good Elementary is in the same district as Poor Me Elementary, but that's all they have in common. At Pretty Good Elementary, there is no rental property. Everyone owns their home and is proud of it. Everyone speaks English and maybe another language just for fun. No one is on free or reduced lunch. There is virtually no mobility. In fact, parents of kindergartners are already requesting the teachers they want their children to have in first, second, or third grade. Almost every home has two parents. No one rides the bus because children walk or ride their bikes safely to school, or neighborhood car pools pick them up on their way to Scouts, soccer practice, or piano lessons. Along the way they will stop and have a snow cone. Life is nice at Pretty Good Elementary, and so are the scores. They are pretty good.

But they are not excellent. Faculty and staff at Pretty Good Elementary have been content with their pretty good scores. After all, they always outperform those poor, pitiful little children over at Poor Me Elementary, God bless them. Here at Pretty Good Elementary, students can do relatively well without too much extra effort. They look good under the State, District, and Campus columns, so what is the problem?

That is where the campus group comes in handy. Now scores from Pretty Good Elementary are being compared with scores from other pretty good elementary schools. Oops! What principal would like to have to explain to their superintendent why, although their scores are at the top of their district, they are below those of other campuses that look virtually just like them? This would not be a happy conference. Therefore, instruction at all the pretty good campuses also becomes more focused. The result is improved curriculum, instruction, and assessment.

The same is true for every school in between. Although some consider the campus group a headache, it is actually a good thing. It keeps all schools on their toes and cognizant of how other schools with similar demographics are doing. The net results are improved learning and accountability for everyone.

The Campus column is, obviously, your own campus's scores. It is the first column you look at. As you prepare for the test by analyzing various AEIS reports—and later when you're a principal—you'll want to highlight this column in yellow to help you focus on it. Every campus stakeholder wants to know how his or her school is doing. These reports are now available per campus and district over the Internet, adding another touch of reality, motivation, and accountability to the situation.

After the Campus column, still thinking "big to little," the columns are divided into various subgroups of students. These include African American, Hispanic, White, Native American, Asian/Pacific Islander, Male, Female, Economically Disadvantaged, and Special Education. The goal is for every subgroup to do well. You do not want to see any large differences in passing rates of students on any section of any test. If you do, you and your school community must ask yourself why, and then create plans and strategies to resolve the discrepancies. In the ideal school, instruction is individualized and curriculum is developmentally appropriate such that there will be no significant deviations between subgroups. When, in reality, there are deviations, intense study and planning is undertaken from many stakeholders to resolve the situation so that all students learn and perform well.

Those are all of the categories placed into columns. Along the left side of each page in Section I will be rows labeled with the subjects tested such as Reading, Math, Writing, or All Tests. Appropriate scores will be noted on two lines, one for the current year and one for the previous year. In each area, you will want your scores to go up annually, not go down. If they are going down or remaining stagnant, you and your school community must analyze why and plan for improvement.

All Tests is an interesting row. It is there to determine the percentage of students who passed every test they took. It is necessary because if you just looked at the individual subjects and compared results, sometimes you could get a less-than-complete picture. For example, let's go back to our hypothetical third-grade class. Assume that 50% of the grade passed reading and 50% passed math. At first glance, you might think, "Well, 50% of the students in third grade are doing really well. The other 50% cannot read or do math."

This could be a wrong conclusion. What if it was a different set of students that passed each portion? What if 50% of them could read *War and Peace,* but couldn't add 2 + 2? What if the other 50% could work algorithms, but could not read *The Cat in the Hat?* Hmm. We have a problem here. That is why we have the *All Tests* row. It allows us to see an overall picture of exactly what percentage of the grade or school is passing everything taken. The goal is to have 100% of the students passing all tests.

The first portion of Section I will always be set up in this format per grade located at that school. Therefore, this is where you would look if you were asked any questions that relate to specific grade level or subgroup performance on any test for any grade. If you are asked to compare scores, ascertain trends, or identify strengths or weaknesses of performance, this is where you would look.

The next portion of Section I is a summary of all the scores in the school or district. The rows and columns of the chart remain the same. It will say TAAS % Passing Sum of 3–8 & 10. If the school you are analyzing does not have all those grades, it doesn't matter. This chart is simply a quick reference guide to the overall performance of how the entire school or district did on the specified subjects and All Tests. If you are asked any questions about overall campus performance, this is where you would look first.

At the bottom of this portion will be an important section labeled TAAS% Exempted Sum of 3–8 & 10. This is important because although it would be wonderful to have 100% passing rates in every category above, if you have exempted half the school, it's not a good sign. Central office people and school boards, as well as the state itself, look closely at this. They do not want you exempting high percentages of students. Their goal is for everyone to test and score well. Therefore, this section will show the percentage of students, per subgroup, that you have exempted for either special education or limited English proficiency purposes. Again, it is very important for you not to have high percentages in this area. This is one of the few places where you want your numbers to be lower than those in the State, District, or Campus Group columns. You particularly do not want high percentages of exemptions within any of your subgroups. Again, the goal is for everyone to test and everyone to do well.

The last portion of Section I is Attendance. Attendance is important because if students are not coming to school, it is difficult for them to learn anything—or at least the things you want them to learn. The same format of groups is also used here. The important thing to notice is that the two years listed are always one year in arrears. That is not an accident, nor is it placed there to confuse you. The reason is simple. This academic year is not over yet; therefore, it is impossible to determine the total percent of attendance. Obviously, you want your attendance percentages to be higher than those in the State, District, or Campus Group columns. You do not want to see high percentage rates among some of your subgroups, whereas one or more are pitiful. If a certain subgroup has low attendance, it is critically important to ascertain why. Why are these students not coming to school? What can we as a school community do to address this situation? If students are not in attendance, it is difficult for them to learn. A major goal of a democratic society is to produce literate, cognizant, contributing citizens. It is difficult to do that when students are not in school.

Section II of an AEIS Report

As mentioned earlier, a simple way to remember what is in Section II is that it includes everything that is not in Section I. Although that may seem obvious, it's easy to remember what is in Section I—testing and attendance. If you are asked a question that does not relate to testing or attendance, go straight to Section II. Remember, if you get lost in an AEIS report, the quickest way to navigate it is to look at the top right-hand corner of each page. It will tell you if you are in Section I or Section II. Now let's see what is in Section II.

The first segment of Section II is Student Information. Everything is still presented in chart format. The subgroups no longer appear. The basic layout will be Campus (including Count and Percent columns), Campus Group, District, and State. You will be given basic enrollment (not testing) information such as how many students and what percentage of enrollment is in each grade at a given school. It will be further disaggregated into Ethnic Distribution, Mobility, Economically Disadvantaged, Limited English Proficient, Number of Students per Teacher, and Retention Rates by Grade. This will be charted in rows comparing your school with your campus group, district, and the state. In general, there is no doing better or worse than the other groups. These are merely facts. Nonetheless, in the segments labeled Number of Students per Teacher, you would like to see a small ratio of students to teachers; in Retention Rates by Grade (for both regular and special education students), you would like to see a small percentage of retention. Although this section does not relate to testing, it is an important place to look when you are analyzing a report. Just as you do not want high passing rates due to high exemption rates (found in Section I), you also do not want high passing rates due to flunking everybody (found in this portion of

Section II). This is the kind of critical thinking that TExES developers want to see if you will catch. Watch for it. You want everyone doing well on TAAS, of course, but not because the school exempted or flunked everyone at risk of not passing. Basically, though, if you are given a question that pertains to enrollment, ethnic distribution, mobility, economically disadvantaged, limited English proficiency, number of students per teacher, or retention rates by grade for either regular or special education students, then the Student Information chart of Section II is where you would look. Remember that on test-taking day.

The next section of Section II is Staff Information. It is set up in the same Campus (Count and Percent), Campus Group, District, and State format as Student Information. This is where you would look to determine the numbers and percentages of staff who are professional (teachers, professional support, and campus administration), plus educational aides, total staff, total minority staff, teachers by ethnicity and gender, teachers by years of experience, average years of experience of teachers, average years of experience of teachers with district, average teacher salary by years of experience, and average actual salaries for teachers, professional support, and campus administration. This information is public information and freely available to any citizen who wants to see it either by hard copy or via the Internet. The AEIS report brings it all together in one place.

If you are asked any questions regarding average salaries for virtually anyone, this is where you would look. If you are asked questions that involve planning for future personnel needs, you could look to see the average years' experience of your staff to begin thinking about future retirements and their potential effect on staffing, the budget, and instruction. This is where you would look to see how well your campus is doing in comparison with the other groups on recruiting and retaining minority staff, which is a pressing issue for all districts. Watch for that common theme to appear on the test.

For virtually any question you may have that relates to staffing, the Staff Information section is where you would look first. Always think, "Is there any place else I could look for something that could be of importance in answering this question?" Remember, the competencies refer to multiple sources of data repeatedly. By becoming familiar with exactly where to find what you're looking for in the AEIS report, you can use multiple pieces of information from within the same document to make an intelligent decision.

The next component in Section II is Budgeted Operating Expenditure Information. This is where you will find everything about the budget in summarized form. The format will again compare the Campus (Count and Percent), Campus Group, District, and State. A general rule of thumb is that superintendents, school boards, and especially taxpayers like your test scores to be higher than anyone else's, but for you to be doing it with less money. Using that rationale, this is the other place in the AEIS report where you would like your numbers to be less than your comparison groups. The first place was in Section I in TAAS % Exempted Sum of 3–8 & 10. We discussed it again in Number of Students per Teacher and Retention Rates by Grade.

When it comes to money, look for prudence. This is particularly true in relation to administrative costs. Boards and taxpayers like to see money targeted directly toward students and instruction and as little as possible toward administration. Within the Budgeted Operating Expenditure Information, you will find the actual amount and percentage of the budget for the Total Campus Budget by Function and Per Pupil. Think, "Scores up. Costs down." Remember that when looking at both budgets and test results, especially on test-taking day.

The last chart in Section II is Program Information. This is where you will find how many students are in each category of campus program as well as the amount of money spent on them. Program Information uses the consistent Section II chart format of columns for Campus (Count and Percent), Campus Group, District, and State. The rows provide the categories. These are Student Enrollment by Program for special education, career & technology education, bilingual/ESL education, and a gifted & talented education. It provides the numbers and percentages of Teachers by Program for regular, special, compensatory, career and technology, bilingual/ESL, gifted and talented, and other. Next, it details the Budgeted Instructional Operating Expenditures by Program for these same categories. If you are asked questions about program equity, particularly in the area of finance, this would be where you would look.

Use common sense—of which there is an uncommon lack!

Summary

In closing our study of data analysis through standardized tests and AEIS reports, remember to do these things:

- Look to see the big picture of what you have been given. What kind of test or what portion of an AEIS report have you been given?
- What concepts or components are provided?
- Do not play the "What If?" game. Do not try to be psychic by trying to draw conclusions about the data before you see the questions. Turn the page and read the questions. Then you will know where to look and what to analyze.
- The test developers are looking only for entry-level data analysis skills. Keep your anxiety level down so your productivity will stay up.
- Practice looking at various standardized test results and AEIS reports within your own district or on the Internet (www.tea.state.tx.us/perfreport/aeis/) before taking the TExES so you will be familiar and comfortable with forms and layout.
- Regarding AEIS reports, memorize what goes in Sections I and II. This will save you time and anxiety on the day of your test.

Assuming that you have one or more decision sets relating to an AEIS report, look to see if you have a Section I, a Section II, or both. Similar to standardized test results, you will look at the big picture of what you have been given. You can easily remember what types of information you will find in Section I. It is basically testing and attendance. Everything else is in Section II. Go directly to the questions to see exactly what they are asking rather than playing the "What If?" game of what they might ask. This saves time and effort.

Knowing and becoming familiar with the format of an AEIS report and knowing what will always be in Sections I and II turns a scary and sometimes formidable portion of TExES into a very workable passage. Remember, Section I has testing and attendance. Everything else is in Section II. Every campus and district has copies of their AEIS readily available for the public to access. You are free to look at your own or any others either in person or on the Internet (www.tea.state.tx.us.prefreport/aeis/). Knowing this and making yourself familiar with multiple AEIS reports from various campuses before the TExES will help you to be able to walk into your test cool, calm, collected, confident, and downright cocky. And that's what you'll be as you ace this test.

Test-Taking Strategies

The developers of the principal TExES assumed that students who are preparing for the examination have had an appropriate university or alternative preparation program in school administration. It is the purpose of this book to build on that foundation and help you pass the TExES. Assuming that you have the prerequisite knowledge base necessary and that you use the philosophy and skills presented in this book, you should *ace* this test. That means you should be able to walk in to take TExES cool, calm, collected, confident, and downright cocky. The test, from this point on, is a mind game. What you think you will achieve, you will achieve. If you think you will pass the test, you will. If you think you will not, you will not. Either way, you will be right.

Bearing that in mind, there are specific strategies that will be helpful. Two of these are games. Thus far, you have studied a lot for TExES. Now it is time to play some games and learn other strategies to help you win this mind game.

The Dot Game: Psychological and Time Management

You will have five hours to answer approximately 125 questions on the test. That's plenty of time. There is no reason for you to run out of time. I have, however, on rare occasion heard of someone who claims he or she did. I am going to teach you how to play a deceptively simple game called the Dot Game. If you play it, there's no way you'll run out of time. Here's how to play.

Each decision set comprises a prompt followed by questions related to it. When you begin the test, you will read the prompt that introduces the first decision set. Remember, there are no questions or answers in the prompt. The prompt simply tells you a little bit about the school or situation the question addresses. As you read, underline words that you think are important. You are allowed to write in your test booklet. You do not get bonus points for turning in a clean test booklet, so use your visual and kinesthetic senses by underlining key words or important concepts while taking the TExES.

After reading the prompt, you will begin reading the first question. You will mark the answer. You will read the next question. You will mark the next answer. This will go along just fine until you get to a question where you really are unsure of the answer. Read it again. If you still do not feel confident, put a dot by the question and move on. Just skip that question. Don't feel guilty, and don't look back. Just put a dot by it and keep moving.

Continue until you hit another question where you are unsure of the answer. Put a dot by it, too. Do not spend more than two minutes pondering the right answer to any question. The longer you spend trying to figure out the answer, the more your anxiety level will go up. When your anxiety level goes up, your productivity goes down. Worse, the clock is ticking. The clock is not your friend. Therefore, put a dot by the question and move on.

Repeat this process throughout the entire test. I don't care if you have 30 dots when come to the end of the test. Big deal. You have accomplished something significant: You have worked your way through the entire test. You know every question and concept on it. The pressure is off.

Here is what I want you to do after finishing your first run of the test. Close your book. Get up. Go to the restroom. Shake out the tension in your muscles. Get a drink of water. Walk around for a minute or two. It will be time well spent to rid your body and mind of tension and stress and loosen up. Then, before you go back, stop and tell yourself out loud, "Thank goodness I have made it through this test the first time. Now I am going back in there to finish acing this baby!" Don't ignore what I'm saying. Your subconscious must hear you affirm that you are going to pass this test. Repeat it over and over, out loud and silently. It is all a part of winning the mind game.

When you go back into the testing room, only return to the questions with dots. You will be pleasantly surprised to see how many of them you can answer quickly this time. There are three reasons for this:

- The pressure is off. You have already seen everything on the test. There is nothing scary left. Psychologically, your subconscious begins to relax.
- You know that in this instance, you do not have to score 100. School districts don't really care what your score is. They only care whether you're certified. A passing score on TExES, plus other certification requirements, will accomplish that goal.
- There is something odd that happens after you have read the entire test. The TExES philosophy, as well as key words and phrases, will settle into your subconscious and become familiar. If you haven't spent too long pondering the questions for which you don't have immediate answers, most of the time, on the second run through, the appropriate answers will quickly come to you. This is not as likely to happen if you spent too long pondering each question.

If you do not have all the answers after your second run through, it's perfectly all right. Repeat the process. Close your book. Take a break, just as you did before. Your anxiety level should be way down by now because you know that you do not need to make 100.

Regardless, keep repeating the Dot Game until you have answered all the questions. If it takes more than three times, guess and go home. You are not penalized for wrong answers. You are not likely to have divine intervention at this point. There is no sense in sitting there forever, pondering a question to which you simply don't know the answer.

If you play the Dot Game, there is no way that you can run out of time. If you do not play the Dot Game, you will lose time and productivity on a few questions, resulting in leaving a stack of easy questions unanswered. While you sit there stewing over question 41, the clock is ticking away. Worse, your chances of getting question 41 correct are going down because your anxiety level is going up. Don't do that. Just play the Dot Game as directed and keep your progress moving.

There are some students who are simply slow readers. The Dot Game is particularly beneficial for them. This test includes a lot of reading. I strongly suggest that slow readers check into taking a reading comprehension or speed-reading course. Regardless, it is imperative that you play the Dot Game to keep moving and focused. You do not want to run out of time while you are still trying to decipher the second decision set.

Finally, in the unlikely event that you play the Dot Game through two or three times and then suddenly fall into a coma until a test monitor comes to shake you awake and tell you it's time to leave, here is what you do: Guess. Guess like crazy, and do it quick before they throw you out. Then go seek medical attention about your coma.

This is the most important thing: Leave no question unanswered. You must put something down to have a chance at getting it right. Any chance beats no chance. If you get it right thanks to blind luck, congratulations.

That, my friends, is how to play the Dot Game. It is deceptively simple. Play it and win. It will help you stay cool, calm, collected, confident, and downright cocky.

The Dog and Star Game: Making Good Choices

The TExES is a multiple-choice test. You do not need to memorize facts. You do need to synthesize and apply the philosophy of the nine competencies as well as the strategies presented here. There will be four answer choices. In the best of times, one of them will shout at you as being correct. That answer is a star. We like stars. They make our lives easy. Still, since you'll be such a good test taker, you want to make sure you're right. Therefore, when you find a really good answer, otherwise known as a star, draw a little star by that response in your booklet. But keep reading. Do you see any more really good answers? If so, mark them too. By process of elimination, one of those stars has to be brighter than the others. That means, in truth, one is a star while another is a starlet. Think to yourself, if I can only pick one of these heavenly bodies, which one will it be? Which one is the brightest? Which one has more of the competency language in it? Which response includes the most "Important Points to Remember"? That response is the star. Mark it.

While we love stars, there is another kind of response that we like just as much. They are dogs. Dogs are bad answers. Why would we be watching for bad answers? Because there are only four response choices. If one of them is a dog, use those good old kinesthetic and visual senses again and draw a great

big line through it. As the test progresses, you will take great pride in draw-
ing big, heavy lines through those dogs. This is important for three reasons:

- Every time you identify a dog, your chances of getting the answer
  right go up by 25%.
- If you can find a dog and a puppy, mark both of them out. You have
  just increased your chances of getting the question right by 50%!
- It is good psychology for you to feel and see the results of your decision-
  making process. It adds to your subconscious confidence that you are
  attacking the test in a methodical way and that you are going to *pass*
  this test out of sheer diligence and conscientiousness. Therefore, be
  sure to draw a line through every answer you know is wrong.

Let's say that out of four potential choices, you did not find a star. However,
as you are reading the responses, you find a starlet, or a pretty good answer. You
are not in love with it, but it'll do. You also found a dog and a puppy. The other
choice is just . . . there. Or, as often happens, it is a perfectly good response. It
just doesn't answer this particular question. The test developers do that a lot.
It tends to confuse people who think, "That's a good thing to do." Well, it may
be. It just doesn't answer this question, and therefore it's a wrong response even
if it is a good thing to do. Always bear in mind what each question is asking.
This is part of why it's important to underline key words or phrases in every
question. It helps to keep you focused on the intent of this question.

If you find a starlet, a puppy, a dog, and a nonissue, your correct answer
is the starlet. It may not have been a bright, shining star, but it'll do. Mark it.
It is the best choice available and will get the job done. We love stars and we
love dogs, but we will settle for starlets and puppies. Each time you can identify any of these, your chances of getting the question correct go up by 25%.
If you can eliminate two, your chances go up by 50%. On occasion, there will
be times when you can eliminate three choices. That's a wonderful thing
because by process of elimination, you now have the correct answer.

Multiple Multiples

As we know, the entire TExES is multiple choice with four selections. There
are some questions that are more complex, however. The test developers
present the question in the standard method. After that, they list four potential solutions prefixed by roman numerals I, II, III, and IV. Under that are the
standard choices A, B, C, and D. The choices for A through D are various
combinations of roman numerals I through IV. It could look like this:

Example: Where does Dr. Wilmore teach?
    I. Texas A&M
   II. UT–Austin
   III. Trinity
   IV. UT–Arlington

A. I, II
B. III, IV
C. I, II, III
D. IV

These multiple multiples drive some people crazy. I must admit that at one time I was against them. I felt they got away from the intent of the test, which is to determine entry-level skills for the principalship. I felt they put too much focus on reading comprehension and test-taking skills. It's not up to me to rewrite the test, though. This is the test as we have it today. We cannot change it, but we sure can pass it. Here's how to beat the multiple multiples.

Do this one with me as an example. I teach at the University of Texas at Arlington. Therefore, we would look at roman numeral I, Texas A&M. Do I teach there? No. Immediately, go straight to the lettered answer choices. Do you see any responses with a "I" for Texas A&M in them? Yes, you do. A and C have a "I" in them. What do we do? Draw a line through A and C. Your chances of getting this question just went up 50% before you even have read the rest of the choices. That, folks, is a good deal. It means we are now down to choices B and D. Therefore, let's keep going. "I" was a dog. Let's see what else we can find.

Our only remaining choices are B and D. Do they have anything in common? Yes, they do. They both have "IV" in them. "IV" is the University of Texas at Arlington. Do I teach at the University of Texas at Arlington? Yes, I do. That confirms for us that our correct choice will be B or D. How do we decide which of these is correct?

Look at B and D. They have "IV" in common. What do they have that is different? B has a "III" in it. D does not.

What is III? Trinity. Therefore, the answer will lie in whether I teach at the University of Texas at Arlington *and* Trinity or just the University of Texas at Arlington. If I teach at both, the appropriate answer is B. If I only teach at the University of Texas at Arlington, the answer is D.

I only teach at the University of Texas at Arlington. Therefore, the answer is D.

Usually, the questions will be less factual than this example. They will require application thinking about learner-centered leadership. Still, you should follow the same process. I will detail it here.

Process to Follow for Multiple Multiples

- Start with the first roman numeral. Ask yourself if it is a possible answer.
- If the answer is yes, go straight to the lettered responses at the bottom (A, B, C, and D). Draw a line through any responses that do not have that answer in it.
- If the answer is no, draw a line through any questions that do have that response in it.

- What do you have left? What do these responses have in common? Can you live with it?
- How are they different?
- Choose the difference you prefer. That's your answer.

Multiple multiples can turn out to be your best friend if you follow this process. Often, there will be a dog, a star, or both within the roman numeral selections. Use them to your advantage. By doing this, often the correct answer will pop out at you, leaving only one possible choice. That is exactly what you want. By the process of elimination using dogs and stars, you can get the right answer without undue headache. Students repeatedly tell me that by following this method, they begin to wish all the questions on the test were multiple multiples. Turn a potentially frightening situation into a positive one by following this process with each roman numeral.

Key Words and Themes

Review Chapters 3 through 11 on the learner-centered competencies. You do not need to memorize them, but read them over and over, slowly, for comprehension and synthesis of their concepts. Think about what they mean. Practice visualizing how you will put them into practice after you pass the test and become a principal. You will see key words and concepts repeated such as *multiple use of data* for a concept and *all* and *facilitate* as words. Sometimes you will even see answer choices that appear almost to quote a competency. When you see answer choices that use the same words or concepts, pick that answer. If the test developers had preferred other concepts, language, or words, they would have used them. Stick with ideas you know they like. That's why they are in the competencies.

The Ideal Principal

The ideal principal always does what's right, even when it is difficult or politically unpopular. Think ideal, then mark the ideal response. Collaborate with everyone on everything. Facilitate and align all students, teachers, parents, and everyone else for maximum productivity and efficiency to ensure continuous student success. You are the ideal principal. You are on a relentless pursuit of excellence for all school community stakeholders. If all else fails, think, "Which one of these crazy choices would Elaine choose?" Then mark it because it is the right answer!

Summary

The Dot Game is a strategy to help you use your time effectively while keeping your anxiety level down and your confidence up. Use it. Repeat the process at will. If you've done it two or three times and still have dots left, mark the responses you think the ideal principal would choose. Remember, this test is not designed for what the average, run-of-the mill principal would do. It is built on a philosophy that all principals want to do the right, moral, and ethical things necessary to produce schools of character in a democratic society. Do not select answers that you think are what is actually done in schools if there is a better choice that reaches to a higher standard of moral or ethical responsibility to the school community.

By playing the Dot Game and the Dog and Star Game, as well as always thinking "ideal," you will make good choices and pass TExES. Once you pass the test, get your certification, and land a great job in school administration, remember that it is your moral and ethical responsibility to do the right thing even when something else would be easier. We are not in this for the easy ride. We are in this to make our world a better place. You are needed. Go forth and do it!

Creating a Personal Success Plan

Having goals is an important thing. John Hoyle of Texas A&M University says there is a funny thing about people who set goals. They tend to reach them. Noted motivational speaker Zig Ziegler's people say that only 2% to 3% of people in the world set goals. Then there is the bumper sticker on a car in Arlington that said, "Goals without deadlines are only dreams." We must set goals and have timelines to achieve them.

You have goals of passing the TExES examination, obtaining principal certification, and becoming an awesome administrator. The first step in that plan is passing the TExES examination. You have the knowledge base. You now are armed with the philosophy necessary to understand and apply the nine learner-centered competencies. You have specific strategies to help you make correct choices on the test. What else can you do to ensure you pass the test?

You can create an individual success plan to meet your specific needs. This personal success plan will be uniquely your own. It will be designed to help you win the mind game of the TExES examination.

Tips for Repeat Test Takers

What if you have taken the test in the past and not passed? Are there things you can do to improve your likelihood this time?

Yes. If you have truly studied, synthesized, and internalized the leadership concepts in this book, you should ace it. Nonetheless, there are some additional things you can do to improve your chances and your confidence. You, of all people, need the benefit of going into this test cool, calm, collected, confident, and downright cocky. I have had numerous people from around the state contact me and say that before attending my preparation classes, they had been unsuccessful in passing TExES. Yet after attending my classes and doing what I suggested to them, they passed the test. Hearing from them makes my day. When they ask me if there is anything they can do to thank me, I remind them that I really like *pink* roses, Blue Bell chocolate ice cream, and Hershey bars—plain with no nuts. You would be surprised how many roses and Hershey bars I've received!

Here are some specific suggestions to help you pass the test.

Application of Competencies.   Go back to each of the nine learner-centered competencies. Read, study, and analyze them slowly for comprehension, not memorization, of the concepts they represent.

- To help you internalize their meaning, develop a portfolio with nine sections. There should be one section for each of the nine competencies. Begin watching administrators around you in various contexts. In your mind, try to associate every positive thing they do with at least one of the competencies. Take notes, collect artifacts, and write brief reflective summaries of each activity. Place the notes into the appropriate section of your competency portfolio. Writing the brief summaries will help you analyze the activity you have observed into its various components.

- Often you will have difficulty deciding if an activity belongs with one or a different competency. That's all right. The principal's job is an integrated position. We are not going to split hairs over what goes where. You will not receive bonus points on the test for knowing exactly which questions go with which competencies. *The important thing is that you are connecting real-life applications with the concepts of the competencies.* You are thus making the competencies come alive. You are internalizing and synthesizing them. When you see scenarios of principal behavior in the TExES questions, you will already be accustomed to analyzing behavior. Your portfolio will help you select the appropriate responses. Your portfolio will be authentic and applied TExES preparation.

- Having someone to collaborate with for this activity will multiply the benefits for both of you. If you have an encouraging mentor, a supportive friend, or even a friendly classmate, ask him or her to take the time once a week to sit down together and walk through your portfolio. It will be particularly beneficial if your partner is preparing for the test, too. Describe orally each artifact, set of notes, and summary. The act of orally describing what they are and why you selected them will manifest itself in critical and reflective thinking, which are, of course, higher-order thinking skills. As the developer of the taxonomy of higher-order thinking skills, Benjamin Bloom would be proud. So will you when you get your passing TExES scores.

Content.   Look at the score sheet or sheets you have received in previous TExES endeavors. Write down your scores per domain rather than your total score. Forget your total score. If you bring up your domain and competency scores, it will automatically bring up your overall score.

- Within your scores, you will have relative strengths, which are your higher scores. You will also have relative weaknesses, which are your lower scores. Target the areas on which you'd like to focus for this test administration. Go back to your college textbooks and notes for those areas. Review them. Study particularly the corresponding chapters of this book that go with those competencies. Study the additional resources that I have suggested per competency. In this way, your preparation will be focused on your greatest needs. You will be working smarter instead of harder.

Reading Comprehension or Speed-Reading Courses or Review. I have been convinced for years that there are many intelligent people who have had bad luck passing TExES because of a combination of factors. Some are not prepared cognitively. They do not have the appropriate knowledge base. Others amazingly have never had the philosophy of learner-centered leadership stressed to them. How can anyone be expected to pass a test without a comprehension of the philosophy on which it is built? Others are lacking in test-taking skills. Some, though, have difficulty with TExES because of the intense amount of reading involved.

- Every decision set and question involves reading, comprehension, analysis, and synthesis for application. Although many test takers are highly intelligent, reading comprehension might not be high on their list of talents. Maybe they can comprehend, but they read very slowly. As they read slowly, time is ticking away. Eventually, panic begins to set in. We know for a fact that panic is counterproductive to passing TExES. When anxiety goes up, productivity goes down. That is not what we want. We want productivity to stay up and anxiety to stay down. Practice deep breathing or yoga relaxation techniques. Only you know if you fit in this category.
- I strongly suggest that you work on your reading comprehension or speed skills. Various organizations, including Sylvan Learning Centers, and university or school district continuing education courses, offer classes in these areas. Another good resource is public school English or reading teachers. They often know of many good books, tapes, or techniques that could benefit you. The public library as well as school and university libraries also will have resources to assist you. I cannot stress enough the importance of reading comprehension in passing this test. If you think you read well but have been unsuccessful in passing the TExES exam more than once, what do you stand to lose?

Tips for Out-Of-State Future Texas Principals

Often there are people from out of state, particularly current administrators, who seek to become principals in Texas. Welcome! We love our state and welcome you to it. Be sure you bring along a firm commitment to learner-centered leadership!

The competency information provided in this book will bring things you have known for years to the forefront of your mind. To my surprise, many of the states adjacent to Texas are not stressing learner-centered leadership. Or, it could be that they are, but you have been out of school for a long time and not actively involved in this type professional development. We can solve that.

It is particularly important for you to think "ideal principal." In many ways, it is more important for you than it is for the nonprincipals taking the test. Remember, this test is designed for entry-level administrative skills. If you have years of experience, you will have a tendency to look at potential responses from an experienced perspective. You know what will or will not work in real life.

Forget real life. Think ideal. If a response may seem a little unrealistic to you but you know that in an ideal school with an ideal principal it likely would happen, mark that answer because it's the right one. The idea here is to lift the benchmark of principal behavior as much as possible, especially with new principals, to the level of ideal. Remember Les Brown, who told us in Chapter 2 to aim for the moon. Even if you miss it, you will land among the stars. We want every principal, new and experienced, to aim for the moon, the epitome of the ideal principal, every day in every way. In so doing, our schools may not reach the top, but they will achieve higher than they currently are. What could be wrong with that?

The last thing I suggest is for you to get on the Internet and study different AEIS reports for various schools. Because AEIS reports are a Texas thing, you may not be familiar with their layout. But you will be familiar with the types of data presented therein. Look up an AEIS report and play with it. Look for good things and bad things in the different ones you find. Every campus and district AEIS report is on the Internet, so you will have easy access (www.tea.state.tx.us/perfreport/aeis). You can decipher AEIS reports, but becoming familiar and comfortable with them ahead of time will save you time and anxiety on the day of your test. You will be able to whiz right through it, playing the Dot Game (see Chapter 13), of course. Remember, *think ideal.*

Now, back to everyone reading this book. What else should you do to prepare yourself cognitively, psychologically, and emotionally?

Mantras

The principal TExES exam is a mind game based on student-centered leadership. The domains and competencies develop and portray this philosophy. In this book, you have studied, processed, and applied them in every conceivable scenario. Cognitively you are prepared. Logically, you should and will pass the test.

What about illogically? What if you are so frightened that you cannot think straight? What if, deep down, you are truly scared you will fail the test? What if your job or future job depends on passing? You cannot think *ideal school* or *ideal principal* because you are too busy breaking out in hives.

You must beat that paradigm. Your mind must be convinced that you will not just pass the TExES, you will ace it. You will do so well that they will audit your results. You will do great and make me proud.

To convince your inner self of that, begin saying out loud, "I am going to ace this test. I am going to do great. I am thinking 'ideal' all day long." Do this 100 times a day from now until you pass. Write it on 50 Post-its and put them everywhere. Each time you see one, read it out loud. Say it with spirit. Practice being calm, cool, collected, confident, and downright cocky. Repeat the mantra ad nausuem. Repeat it alone, in public, in boring meetings, in your car, and while exercising or shopping. Sing it in the shower. Repeat it until you drive those around you crazy. Keep repeating it as you take the test. You are what you believe you are. You are a success. You are going to make a real difference in this world. Believe it. Do it. You will be great!

From Now Until Test-Taking Week

From now till the test, review Section II of this book every week. Study the competencies. Read through them slowly as you focus on the concepts they represent. Do not attempt to memorize anything, but do focus on the terms, language, and common themes that emerge. Once a week read Chapters 2 through 11 for review. I do not want you to think, "Well, I read the book so I am ready for the test." That's nice, and you may pass the test, but you do need to prepare, integrate, synthesize, apply, and not forget all I have been preaching to you about these competencies.

By reading the competencies over and over until you are sick of them and never want to see them again, you will become as familiar and comfortable with them and the concepts they represent as you currently are with driving to school. Driving to school may not be a big deal to you because you do it every day. But remember when you were first learning to drive? Driving anywhere was a big deal. You watched every corner, every traffic light, and likely gripped the steering wheel when other cars came your way.

Think of these competencies as learning to drive. I want you so thoroughly familiar and comfortable with them that when you take the TExES they will seem as natural as driving to school. You are the driver of this test. Drive it well.

The Week of the Test

You have prepared religiously. You have read Section II at least once a week until the week of the test. It is now time to get more intense. Reread the entire book. Focus this time on Section III with its strategies and techniques for success. Then each night before you go to bed, read through the competencies again. Let it be the last thing you do before you turn off the lights. Research says the last thing you have on your mind before falling asleep stays in your mind all night long. That is exactly where we want this information to be. We want it working its way through your mind while you sleep, eat, work, and bathe.

As before, read for comprehension, not memorization. By reading them this many times, key words and phrases that appear on the test, especially in answers, will jump right out at you as if they were in bold print. That is good. Those are stars. Mark them. We know if the test developers had liked other words or phrases better, they would have used them. When they use their own language, they are giving you the answer. Take them up on it and say, "Oh! Thank you!"

The Night Before the Test

The night before the test is similar to the last minutes of the test if you are still sitting there. If you are not familiar by that point with the competencies and test-taking strategies presented here, it is not going to come to you by osmosis or divine intervention. Nonetheless, I have, however, had more than one student promise me that prayer works. I am a big believer in prayer myself. I pray for all my students before they test. Maybe that is why they do so well. From this point on, consider yourself my student.

In truth, this is what I want you to do. You will test on a Saturday. On the Friday before you test, come home from school or wherever and relax. Go out to dinner. Take in a movie that is light and fun with pure mindless drivel. Tonight you want mindless drivel. You want absolutely nothing stressful going on. Talk to your family or friends ahead of time. Make sure they understand the importance of your having a calm night. If the cat has kittens, let someone else tend to them. As far as I'm concerned, I don't even want you to know about it.

Go home and relax. Go out to dinner some place you like. Take in a fun, relaxing movie. Come home. Take a nice, hot bath. Then go to bed. You may read through the competencies one last time, but if you don't know them by now, cramming won't help. Read through them, turn off the lights, and say your prayers. The party is over.

The Morning of the Test

Set your clock to get up in plenty of time, particularly if you are assigned a morning test administration. You don't want to be rushed and throwing away all that good relaxation from last night. Leave yourself plenty of time to get ready.

Eat something. Even if you are not a breakfast person, eat something anyway. People who have something in their stomachs to fuel their bodies perform better. You want to have peak performance. This is the Olympics for you. Don't you know all those athletes have specially designed meals to ensure peak performance? You may not have a nutritionist at your house, but you do have cereal and milk, if nothing else.

Dress comfortably. This includes your shoes. You do not need aching feet during the TExES. If you decide your feet hurt during the test, shed the shoes. Dress in layers. I have had multiple students around the entire state complain that the testing sites are really cold. If you dress in layers, you can shed them if you're warm. There is nothing worse than being cold during a test. Also, some people respond to stress by sweating. Others experience slowing of their blood pressure and get cold. By dressing in layers, you will be prepared for either situation. If you have a lucky charm, wear it.

Arrive at the test site early. You don't want to be rushed or to take any chances with traffic, wrecks, emergencies, and so forth. There will be a large number of other test takers there. Most of them will not be taking the same test as you. The lengths of different tests vary, so do not be surprised or chagrined if people sitting around you get up and leave before you are finished. Do not assume that they are innately brilliant and that you are a bump on a pickle. This isn't true. You are the one who is innately brilliant and extremely well prepared. They may be taking a different test or they have guessed their way all the way through the principal test and are hoping for a computer miracle during grading. You take care of your own business, which is also called acing this test.

Remember to play the Dot Game. Both your body and your mind need the break. You reviewed everything about the Dot Game the week before the test. Apply what you know. It is a well-seasoned game and has far greater validity than the lottery. Use the Dog and Star Game. Work your way through the test two or three times, and then hang it up. Remember, you do not have to make 100 on this test. You have been well prepared. You have answered every question. You have given it your all. You are done. Go home!

After the Test

Celebrate! Although most people think they leave the testing site brain dead simply due to the length of the test, you will also know in your heart that you passed it. You will have a deep sense of accomplishment. You will feel an even greater sense of accomplishment the day you get your scores in the mail. But until then, there is not one more thing you can do except celebrate. You deserve it. If you want to see an action thriller tonight, go do it. If you want to run a marathon, go do it. If you want to eat your weight in chocolate, invite me. But whatever you do, do it because it is something that fills your soul with joy. You have accomplished a major goal. You have taken and passed the principal TExES exam. You may not have your scores yet, but you know something that the computer doesn't yet. You won the mind game!

So where are my pink roses, Blue Bell, and Hershey bars?

Go forth and make every day all you can. Make a difference in the life of at least one person every day. Change the world, one school at a time. Join my journey for victory.

From Now Until Eternity

Once you receive your passing scores in the mail, you are done with the TExES. After the celebrating, however, there are a few things left for you to do to obtain your principal certification. You will need to officially apply for state certification with the State Board for Educator Certification (SBEC). You can do this through the certification office at your university or alternative preparation program. Their endorsement of your application is required. There will be a certification fee. Do not forget this important step. Without it, you are not certified. If you are an out-of-state test taker, contact the SBEC directly (State Board of Educator Certification, 1002 Trinity, Austin, TX 78701-2603; Tel. 888-863-5880; www.sbec.state.tx.us).

During the time it takes the SBEC to process your paperwork, you are not officially certified, but you are "certifiable," which means you are eligible to be employed as a certified administrator. The school district may require you to present evidence of your certifiability, which your university will be pleased to provide. Usually a simple letter stating your status on official university letterhead will suffice. Certifications are now provided on-line so both you and your school district can track your progress. It is a wonderful thing when you see your certification appear by your name on-line. Print it out, and show it off to everyone you see.

Go Change the World!

You could very well become employed as an administrator before your certification becomes official. In fact, with the growing shortage of certified administrators both in Texas and around the nation, it is entirely possible that you will become an administrator before you even take the test. You are still required to take and pass it. Study and prepare!

In the end, certification is more than a necessary step to your long-term employment as a school administrator. Meeting all certification requirements through course work, practicums or internships, and the TExES are all designed for one purpose. That purpose is to help you be the best principal on the face of this Earth. Nothing less will do. Is it a competition to be the best principal? Of course not. We want every school to be absolutely outstanding, where every student learns and learns well. Until that happens, we are not finished with our journey toward the ideal. It is absolutely necessary that you aim for being the best principal your campus, your school community, your district, and your world has ever seen. That is what it will take to change and improve our world, one school at a time. Start with yours.

Will it be a daunting task? Yes, it will. Will you become tired, frustrated, and totally disgusted with bureaucracy? Yes, at times you will. But will it also be the most challenging and personally rewarding job you could ever imagine? Without a doubt. There will be tears of fatigue and frustration, but there will also be tears of joy and elation. There will be times you want to beat your head against a wall. But there will also be times of jumping up and down internally and externally over something magnificent that has happened, something that those with lesser faith said could not be done. Yet you knew that it could. You knew that it could because there was nothing on this Earth that was going to make you give up in your continuing quest to change the world, one school at a time.

You have passed the TExES and are headed into your future with anticipation, hope, joy, courage, perseverance, and a little bit of fear. May every day of your journey be blessed. Go forth and make me proud. Change the world. Make it a better place. Together, we can be the difference. Will you join me as we try?

Appendix

Mini Practice Test

Elizabeth Barnes is the new principal of Colin Powell Middle School. Powell has a reputation for being a rough campus. There was a 21% mobility rate among students moving in and out last year, basically due to a large set of federally subsidized apartments located within its attendance zone. A sizeable number of fights and other disruptions among students occur each day on campus, as well as after school in the apartment complex. Although the campus barely received an acceptable rating from the Texas Education Association last year, Ms. Barnes notices that there appears to be no expectation within the school community for improving the behavior or academic performance of students.

1. Ms. Barnes wants to do a good job at Powell, but she is quite concerned about the low expectations the school community displays. What step should she take *first*?
   A. Ask the superintendent what to do.
   B. Demand copies of lesson plans immediately to study and correct their flaws.
   C. Discuss her concerns with the campus leadership team.
   D. Tell the faculty they must crack down on student behavior to get the school under control.

2. Upon investigation, Ms. Barnes discovers that although a site-based decision-making team exists, the committee did not meet at all during the previous year. She is concerned that the lack of input from the school community may be a contributing factor to problems at Powell. To further analyze her hypothesis, Ms. Barnes _____
   A. invites committee members to meet with her immediately to discuss plans for how to proceed.
   B. implements a survey for school and community input.
   C. calls the former principal, who was transferred, to ask for help.
   D. holds a community meeting and invites the mayor and city council.

3. Ms. Barnes is pleased when various stakeholders in the school community express interest in being part of a newly developed Powell Campus Improvement Committee. She is less pleased, however, when a quarrelsome community person who does not have a child at Powell says he wants to be on the committee. She should _____

   A. invite him to join the committee.
   B. call the police.
   C. tell him there are no openings at this time, but as one occurs she will let him know.
   D. tell him membership is reserved for Powell parents.

4. Gradually, a spirit of campus unity begins to emerge. Through extensive collaboration, a shared campus vision is developed. Just as Ms. Barnes is beginning to feel hopeful, two Powell students are arrested for armed robbery and car theft over the weekend. The media broadcast the news. On Monday morning, it appears to be the favorite campus topic of conversation. Ms. Barnes should _____
   A. direct her secretary to hold all calls.
   B. immediately address the issue with the campus to dispel rumors.
   C. hope people will stop talking about it by third period.
   D. question friends of the arrested students as to their weekend activities.

5. The Powell Campus Improvement Committee recommends that higher standards for academic performance be set. Teachers are uncertain how to set realistic goals. Ms. Barnes suggests an analysis of various sources of test data. Good reasons for them to do this include being able to _____
   I. see how students perform collectively and individually on different types of tests.
   II. view demographic subgroups performance.
   III. impress the superintendent.
   IV. look at student performance from varying perspectives.
       A. I, II
       B. II, III
       C. III
       D. I, II, IV

6. Alvin Washington is principal of Thomas Edison Elementary School. Students are predominately from single-family residences located close to the school, although there are a few bus routes. Edison is known for its warm, welcoming climate and high academic expectations. Parental involvement and campus pride runs high. Because of high district growth, the school board decides to redraw attendance zones. This will affect Edison.

Many Edison parents are anxious to hear if the rezoning will affect their children. They intentionally bought homes in the Edison attendance zone so that their children could attend this campus. Mr. Washington does not want to let the situation get out of hand. He should _____

A. call a parents' meeting immediately to assure them that their children will not be moved.
B. talk to the central administration office to see if his campus can be exempted from the rezoning because the parents are upset.
C. meet with teachers, parents, and other community members to come up with a plan to address how the situation will be handled.
D. Direct parents to contact school-board members.

7. Amid all the controversy, Mr. Washington wants to keep teachers and students focused on teaching and learning. A group of fifth-grade teachers approaches him about hosting an academic fair on campus. They are excited about the idea of students doing independent work on language arts, math, science, social studies, and fine arts projects. They want to know if Mr. Washington will allow them to proceed with their plans. Considering the situation, Mr. Washington should _____

A. tell them that it sounds like a good idea and that they can go forward.
B. refer the idea to the campus decision-making team to see if it is in congruence with identified campus goals and objectives.
C. tell them that due to the current situation, it may not be a good idea to host something so enticing because it could further upset the parents whose children may be transferred.
D. see if there are adequate resources to fund the fair.

8. Before the school year is over, attendance rezoning is announced. As expected, some Edison children will be transferred to other campuses. Emotions are running high among parents. Some are happy that their children will continue to attend Edison. Others are unhappy that their children will be moved. What should Mr. Washington do to facilitate a smooth transition for all students?

   I. Work collaboratively with principals where various Edison students will be transferred to accommodate an easy transition.
   II. Form a committee with other principals to tell the superintendent that this really is not such a good idea.
   III. See if there are any ways to get around the rules so more of his students can stay.
   IV. Present a positive image of the rezoning project as an opportunity for everyone to get to know new people and have new experiences.

   A. I, III   C. II, III
   B. I, III, IV   D. I, IV

9. When the new attendance zones are studied, Mr. Washington learns that a large number of students who will be transferred into Edison have limited English proficiency. This was not the case in the past. Mr. Washington is concerned about meeting the needs of his new students. He should consider _____

   A. telling the superintendent that there has been a mistake. His campus does not offer English as a second language (ESL) or bilingual instruction.
   B. demanding additional resources including ESL and bilingual staff.
   C. withdrawing existing programs to allow for new ones.
   D. facilitating organizational decision making and problem solving to address the issue.

Isabella Martinez is the principal of Northwest High School in a large urban district. For the past several years, there have been conflicts and accusations about how cheerleaders are selected. The cheerleader sponsor has been accused of picking her favorites or selecting students from prominent families. Furthermore, there have been accusations that the uniform fund is being mishandled. Ms. Martinez feels these rumors and assertions are contrary to campus productivity. She encourages the site-based decision-making team to address the situation.

10. Ms. Martinez asks the sponsor to provide the set of judging criteria for cheerleader selection. She learns this document does not exist. The sponsor says that she has been doing this job for 15 years and has always let the judges decide. Ms. Martinez _____

    A. recommends that criteria be developed.
    B. says as long as the judges are from out of town and do not know the candidates, the current system is fine.
    C. reprimands the sponsor and removes her from her duties.
    D. thanks the sponsor for her continuing commitment to the squad.

11. After looking at the uniform account, Ms. Martinez notices a wide range of entries and withdrawals that do not appear to be documented. She approaches the sponsor for an explanation. She learns that since the sponsor is so busy, she has been letting various mothers of the girls handle the account. Ms. Martinez _____

    A. congratulates the sponsor for encouraging parental involvement.
    B. recommends the sponsor select just one parent to handle the money to keep the books consistent.
    C. directs the sponsor to provide an accounting of all transactions from this account.
    D. asks a business teacher to implement an accounting plan for cheerleader money as a class project.

12. When report cards are distributed, one of the cheerleaders has a grade of 68 in algebra, which means she cannot participate on the squad until her grade improves. She has asked the algebra teacher to change the grade, but he refused. The cheerleader approaches Ms. Martinez, asking to be allowed to continue cheering, especially for homecoming. Ms. Martinez _____
   A. goes to the teacher to inquire about bonus credits.
   B. tells the student she cannot cheer.
   C. helps the student find an algebra tutor and tells her that if she passes the test tomorrow she can cheer.
   D. tells the student that she will allow her to cheer for homecoming only.

Barbara Watson is principal of the Newcomers Academy in a large urban district. Secondary students who have recently arrived in the United States and who speak no English often begin their studies at the academy. Attendance is sporadic, because many of the students also have jobs to help support their families. Few extracurricular activities are available because of low student interest. Ms. Watson wants to increase school attendance through the development of programs that will be relevant and interesting to the students.

13. The faculty members are against the development of after-school activities at the academy. They say their days are completely full as it is, that they are tired at the end of the day, and that there is no interest among students anyway. What should Ms. Watson do?
   I.   Abandon the idea since the faculty members are against it.
   II. Tell the faculty that she is open to their suggestions as to how to better address the attendance issue.
   III. Conduct a survey among both faculty and students to learn what activities they would like to discuss and potentially develop.
   IV. Ask for volunteers to steer a committee to brainstorm, study, and report on ways to improve attendance and promote school involvement.
      A. I, II
      B. II, III
      C. III, IV
      D. II, III, IV

14. Due to state funding issues, the central administrative office has put pressure on all campuses to improve attendance. The Newcomers Academy decides they would like to change the time of day when official attendance is calculated. They _____
   A. decide to change it to first period because students tend to leave early to get to their jobs.
   B. agree to average the attendance per class period.

    C. research the legalities of changing the time at all.

    D. Reward students who have perfect attendance at the appropriate time each day.

15. Ms. Watson and the faculty survey students to learn ways to increase student attendance. They learn that the students do not feel their curriculum is relevant to their needs. They decide to _____

    A. tell the district curriculum personnel that they do not like their current books and want new ones.

    B. explain to students that their courses are what the state mandates and therefore they cannot be changed.

    C. involve students in planning ways to connect what they are learning at school with their jobs and daily lives.

    D. begin teaching all subjects in the students' native languages.

Answers

1. C	6. C	11. C
2. A	7. B	12. B
3. A	8. D	13. D
4. B	9. D	14. C
5. D	10. A	15. C

Additional Resources

Domain I: School Community Leadership

Banks, J. A., & Banks, C. M. (1996). *Multicultural education: Issues and perspectives.* Boston: Allyn & Bacon.

Bennis, W. (1989). *On becoming a leader.* Reading, MA: Perseus.

Bennis, W. (1989). *Why leaders can't lead.* San Francisco: Jossey-Bass.

Bennis, W. (1999). *Old dogs, new tricks.* Provo, UT: Executive Excellence.

Blanchard, K., & Bowles, S. (1998). *Gung-ho! Turn on the people in any organization.* New York: William Morrow.

Blanchard, K., Hybels, B., & Hodges, P. (1999). *Leadership by the book: Tools to transform your workplace.* New York: William Morrow.

Blanchard, K., & Johnson, S. (1981). *The one minute manager.* New York: Berkley.

Blanchard, K., Oncken, W., Jr., & Burrows, H. (1989). *The one minute manager meets the monkey.* New York: William Morrow.

Blanchard, K., & Peale, N. V. (1988). *The power of ethical management.* New York: Fawcett Columbine.

Blanchard, K., Zigarmi, P., & Zigmari, D. (1985). *Leadership and the one minute manager.* New York: Morrow.

Bolman, L., & Terrence D. (1995). *Path to school leadership.* Thousand Oaks, CA: Corwin.

Brown, G., & Irby, B. (1997). *The principal portfolio.* Thousand Oaks, CA: Corwin.

Bucher, R. D. (2000). *Diversity consciousness: Opening our minds to people, cultures, and opportunities.* Upper Saddle River, NJ: Prentice Hall.

Burton, V. R. (2000). *Rich minds, rich rewards.* Dallas, TX: Pearl.

Covey, S. R. (1990). *Principle-centered leadership.* New York: Simon & Schuster.

Covey, S. R. (1990). *The seven habits of highly effective people.* New York: Simon & Schuster.

Covey, S. R., Merrill, A. R., & Merrill, R. R. (1994). *First things first.* New York: Simon & Schuster.

Daresh, J., & Palyco, M. (1999). *Beginning the principalship*. Thousand Oaks, CA: Sage.

Deal, T. E., & Peterson, K. D. (1994). *The leadership paradox*. San Francisco: Jossey-Bass.

Deal, T. E., & Peterson, K. D. (1999). *Shaping school culture: The heart of leadership*. San Francisco: Jossey-Bass.

De Pree, M. (1989). *Leadership is an art*. New York: Dell.

De Pree, M. (1997). *Leading without power: Finding hope in serving community*. San Francisco: Jossey-Bass.

Drucker Foundation. (1996). *The leader of the future*. San Francisco: Jossey-Bass.

Dyer, K. M. (2000). *The intuitive principal*. Thousand Oaks, CA: Corwin.

English, F. W. (1994). *Theory in educational administration*. New York: HarperCollins.

Hahn, H., & Stout, R. (1994). *The Internet complete reference*. Berkeley, CA: Osborne McGraw-Hill.

Hesselbein, F., Goldsmith, M., & Beckhard, R. (1996). *The leader of the future*. San Francisco: Jossey-Bass.

Hoyle, J. (1995). *Leadership and futuring: Making visions happen*. Thousand Oaks, CA: Corwin.

Hoyle, J. H., English, F., & Steffy, B. (1998). *Skills for successful 21st century school leaders*. Arlington, VA: American Association of School Administrators.

Johnson, S. (1998). *Who moved my cheese?* New York: Putnam.

Josephson, M. S., & Hanson, W. (1998). *The power of character*. San Francisco: Jossey-Bass.

Jossey-Bass. (2000). *The Jossey-Bass reader on educational leadership*. San Francisco: Author.

Kemerer, F., & Walsh, J. (2000). *The educator's guide to Texas school law* (5th ed.). Austin: University of Texas Press.

Kozol, J. (1992). *Savage inequalities: Children in America's schools*. New York: Harper Perennial Library.

Kozol, J. (2000). *Ordinary resurrections: Children in the years of hope*. New York: Crown.

Krzyzewski, M., & Phillips, D. T. (2000). *Leading with the heart: Coach K's successful strategies for basketball, business, and life*. New York: Warner Business Books.

Ledeen, M. A. (1999). *Machiavelli on modern leadership*. New York: St. Martin's Press.

Lunenburg, F. C., & Ornstein, A. C. (2000). *Educational administration: Concepts and practices* (3rd ed.). Belmont, CA: Wadsworth/Thomas Learning.

Marshall, C. (Ed.). (1993). *The new politics of race and gender*. Bristol, PA: Falmer Press.

Miskell, J. R., & Miskell, V. (1993). *Motivation at work*. Homewood, IL: Richard C. Irwin.

Peters, T., & Waterman, R. H. (1993). *In search of excellence.* New York: Warner Books.

Podesta, C. (2001). *Self esteem and the 6-second secret.* Newbury Park, CA: Corwin.

Ramsey, R. D. (1999). *Lead, follow, or get out of the way.* Thousand Oaks, CA: Corwin.

Reinhartz, J., & Beach, D. M. (2001). *Foundations of educational leadership: Changing schools, changing roles.* Boston: Allyn & Bacon.

Schlechty, P. C. (2001). *Shaking up the school house.* San Francisco: Jossey-Bass.

Schmieder, J. H., & Cairns, D. (1996). *Ten skills of highly effective principals.* Lancaster, PA: Technomic.

Schumaker, D. R., & Sommers, W. A. (2001). *Being a successful principal: Riding the wave of change without drowning.* Thousand Oaks, CA: Corwin.

Sergiovanni, T. J. (1992). *Moral leadership: Getting to the heart of school improvement.* San Francisco: Jossey-Bass.

Sergiovanni, T. J. (1996). *Leadership for the schoolhouse.* San Francisco: Jossey-Bass.

Sergiovanni, T. J. (2000). *The lifeworld of leadership.* San Francisco: Jossey-Bass.

Sergiovanni, T. J. (2001). *The principalship: A reflective practice perspective* (4th ed.). Needham Heights, MA: Allyn & Bacon.

Sergiovanni, T. J., & Starratt, R. J. (1998). *Supervision: A redefinition* (6th ed.). Boston: McGraw-Hill.

Short, P. M., & Greer, J. T. (1997). *Leadership in empowered schools: Themes from innovative efforts.* Upper Saddle River, NJ: Prentice Hall.

Starratt, R. J. (1995). *Leaders with vision.* Thousand Oaks, CA: Corwin.

Thomson, S. (Ed.). (1993). *Principals of our changing schools: Knowledge and skill base.* Alexandria, VA: National Policy Board for Educational Administration.

Useem, M. (1998). *The leadership moment.* New York: Times Books.

Warner, C. (1994). *Promoting your school: Going beyond PR.* Thousand Oaks, CA: Corwin.

Whitaker, T. A., Whitaker, B., & Lumpa, D. (2000). *Motivating & inspiring teachers: The educational leader's guide for building staff morale.* Larchmont, NY: Eye on Education.

Domain II: Instructional Leadership

Anderson, J. W. (2001). *The answers to questions that teachers most frequently ask.* Thousand Oaks, CA: Corwin.

Banks, J. A., & Banks, C. M. (1996). *Multicultural education: Issues and perspectives.* Boston: Allyn & Bacon.

Barker, C. L., & Searchwell, C. J. (1998). *Writing meaningful teacher evaluations—right now!!* Thousand Oaks, CA: Corwin.

Barker, C. L., & Searchwell, C. J. (2001). *Writing year-end teacher improvement plans—right now!!* Thousand Oaks, CA: Corwin.

Beach, D. M., & Reinhartz, J. (2000). *Supervisory leadership*. Boston: Allyn & Bacon.

Beane, J. A. (1997). *Curriculum integration: Designing the core of democratic education*. New York: Teachers College Press.

Bennis, W. (1999). *Old dogs, new tricks*. Provo, UT: Executive Excellence.

Bigge, M. L., & Shermis, S. S. (1999). *Learning theories for teachers* (6th ed.). New York: Addison-Wesley Longman.

Blanchard, K. (1998). *Gung ho! Turn on the people in any organization*. Fairfield, NJ: William Morrow.

Blasé, J., & Kirby, P. C. (1992). *Bringing out the best in teachers: What effective principals do*. Newbury Park, CA: Corwin.

Bocchino, R. (1999). *Emotional literacy: To be a different kind of smart*. Thousand Oaks, CA: Corwin.

Brock, B. L., & Grady, M. L. (2000). *Rekindling the flame*. Thousand Oaks, CA: Corwin.

Bucher, R. D. (2000). *Diversity consciousness: Opening our minds to people, cultures, and opportunities*. Upper Saddle River, NJ: Prentice Hall.

Burton, V. R. (2000). *Rich minds, rich rewards*. Dallas, TX: Pearl Books.

Carbo, M. (2000). *What every principal should know about teaching reading*. Syosset, NY: National Reading Styles Institute.

Costa, A. L., & Garmston, R. J. (1994). *Cognitive coaching*. Norwood, MA: Christopher-Gordon.

Creighton, T. B. (2000). *The educator's guide for using data to improve decision making*. Thousand Oaks, CA: Corwin.

Crow, G. M., & Matthews, L. J. (1998). *Finding one's way: How mentoring can lead to dynamic leadership*. Thousand Oaks, CA: Corwin.

Danielson, C., & McGreal, T. L. (2000). *Teacher evaluation to enhance professional practice*. Princeton, NJ: Educational Testing Service.

Erlandson, D. A., Stark, P. L., & Ward, S. M. (1996). *Organizational oversight: Planning and scheduling for effectiveness*. Larchmont, NY: Eye on Education.

Funkhouser, C. W. (2000). *Education in Texas: Policies, practices, and perspectives* (9th ed.). Upper Saddle River, NJ: Prentice Hall.

Gagne, R. M., Briggs, L. J., & Wager, W. W. (1992). *Principles of instructional design* (3rd ed.). New York: Holt, Rinehart and Winston.

Glanz, J. (1998). *Action research: An educational guide to school improvement*. Norwood, MA: Christopher-Gordan.

Glatthorn, A. A. (2000). *The principal as curriculum leader*. Thousand Oaks, CA: Corwin.

Glenn, H. S., & Brock, M. L. (1998). *7 strategies for developing capable students*. Roseville, CA: Prima.

Hadaway, N., Vardell, S. M., & Young, T. (2001). *Literature-based instruction with English language learners*. Boston: Allyn & Bacon.

Hoffman, C., & Ness, J. (1998). *Putting sense into consensus: Solving the puzzle of making team decisions.* Tacoma, WA: VISTA Associates.

Holcomb, E. L. (1998). *Getting excited about data: How to combine people, passion, and proof.* Thousand Oaks, CA: Corwin.

Hoy, W. H., & Miskel, C. G. (1996). *Educational administration: Theory, research, and practice* (5th ed.). New York: McGraw-Hill.

Hoyle, J. R. (1995). *Leadership and futuring: Making visions happen.* Thousand Oaks, CA: Corwin.

Hoyle, J. R., English, F., & Steffy, B. (1998). *Skills for successful 21st century school leaders.* Arlington, VA: American Association of School Administrators.

Irby, B. J., & Brown, G. (2000). *The career advancement portfolio.* Thousand Oaks, CA: Corwin.

Joyce, B., & Weil, M. (1996). *Models of teaching.* Needham Heights, MA: Simon & Schuster.

Kemerer, F., & Walsh, J. (2000). *The educator's guide to Texas school law* (5th ed.). Austin: University of Texas Press.

Kirschmann, R. E. (1996). *Educational administration: A collection of case studies.* Englewood Cliffs, NJ: Prentice Hall.

Marshall, C. (Ed.). (1993). *The new politics of race and gender.* Bristol, PA: Falmer Press.

Maxwell, J. C. (1995). *Developing the leaders around you.* Nashville, TN: Thomas Nelson.

McNamara, J. F., Erlandson, D. A., & McNamara, M. (1999). *Measurement and evaluation: Strategies for school improvement.* Larchmont, NY: Eye on Education.

Merseth, K. K. (1997). *Case studies in educational administration.* New York: Addison-Wesley.

Oliva, P. F. (1997). *Supervision in today's schools* (5th ed.). New York: John Wiley.

Palestini, R. H. (1999). *Educational administration: Leading with mind and heart.* Lancaster, PA: Technomic.

Payne, R. K. (1998). *A framework for understanding poverty.* Baytown, TX: RFT Publishing.

Podesta, C. (2001). *Self-esteem and the 6-second secret.* Newbury Park, CA: Corwin.

Podesta, C., & Sanderson, V. (1999). *Life would be easy if it weren't for other people.* Thousand Oaks, CA: Corwin.

Pratt, D. (1994). *Curriculum planning: A handbook for professionals.* Ft. Worth, TX: Harcourt Brace College.

Reinhartz, J., & Beach, D. M. (2001). *Foundations of educational leadership: Changing schools, changing roles.* Boston: Allyn & Bacon.

Reinhartz, J., & Van Cleaf, D. (1986). *Teach-practice-apply: The TPA instruction model, K-8*. Washington, DC: National Education Association.

Sergiovanni, T. J. (2001). *The principalship: A reflective practice perspective* (4th ed.). Needham Heights, MA: Allyn & Bacon.

Sergiovanni, T. J., & Starratt, R. J. (1998). *Supervision: A redefinition* (6th ed.). Boston: McGraw-Hill.

Sharp, W. L., Walter, J. K., & Sharp, H. M. (1998). *Case studies for school leaders: Implementing the ISLLC standards*. Lancaster, PA: Technomic.

Skrla, L., Erlandson, D. A., Reed, E. M., & Wilson, A. P. (2001). *The emerging principalship*. Larchmont, NY: Eye on Education.

Snowden, P. E., & Gorton, R. A. (1998). *School leadership and administration: Important concepts, case studies, and simulations* (5th ed.). New York: McGraw-Hill.

Thomson, S. (Ed.). (1993). *Principals of our changing schools: Knowledge and skill base*. Alexandria, VA: National Policy Board for Educational Administration.

Weil, J., Weil B., & Weil, M. (1998). *Models of teaching* (6th ed.). Needham Heights, MA: Simon & Schuster.

Whitaker, T. (1999). *Dealing with difficult teachers*. Larchmont, NY: Eye on Education.

Whitaker, T. A., Whitaker, B., & Lumpa, D. (2000). *Motivating & inspiring teachers: The educational leader's guide for building staff morale*. Larchmont, NY: Eye on Education.

Worthen, B., Sanders, J., & Fitzpatrick, J. (1996). *Program evaluation, alternative approaches and practical guidelines* (2nd ed.). New York: Addison-Wesley.

Domain III: Administrative Leadership

Bennis, W. (1997). *Managing people is like herding cats*. Provo, UT: Executive Excellence.

Burrup, P. E., Brimpley, V., Jr., & Garfield, R. R. (1998). *Financing education in a climate of change* (7th ed.). Boston: Allyn & Bacon.

Fitzwater, I. (1996). *Time management for school administrators*. Rockport, MA: Pro-Active.

Fowler, L. S., Henslee, D. G., Fowler, R. P., & Lee, S. M. (2000). *How it works: School construction and technology in Texas* (3rd ed.). Austin, TX: Leap Year.

Fowler, L., Henslee, D. G., & Hepworth, R. D. (1998). *How it works: The Texas school principals complete legal reference system*. Austin, TX: Leap Year.

Funkhouser, C.W. (2000). *Education in Texas: Policies, practices, and perspectives* (9th ed.). Upper Saddle River, NJ: Merrill Prentice Hall.

Henslee, D. G., & Ryan, D. P. (1989). *The Texas principal's handbook*. Austin: Texas School Law News.

Kemerer, F., & Walsh, J. (2000). *The educator's guide to Texas school law* (5th ed.). Austin: University of Texas Press.

McGee-Cooper, A. (1994). *Time management for unmanageable people.* New York: Bantam Books.

Odden, A. R., & Picus, L. O. (1992). *School finance: A policy perspective.* New York: McGraw Hill.

Podesta, C., & Sanderson, V. (1999). *Life would be easy if it weren't for other people.* Thousand Oaks, CA: Corwin.

Smith, H. W. (1994). *The 10 natural laws of successful time and life management.* New York: Warner Books.

Sperry, D. J. (1999). *Working in a legal and regulatory environment: A handbook for school leaders.* Larchmont, NY: Eye on Education.

Walker, B., & Casey, D. T. (1996). *The basics of Texas public school finance* (6th ed.). Austin: Texas Association of School Boards.

**CORWIN
PRESS**